THE YEAR WERE BO

1944

A fascinating book about the year 1944 with information on:
Events of the year UK, Adverts of 1944, Cost of living, Births, Deaths, Sporting events,
Book publications, Movies, Music, World events and People in power.

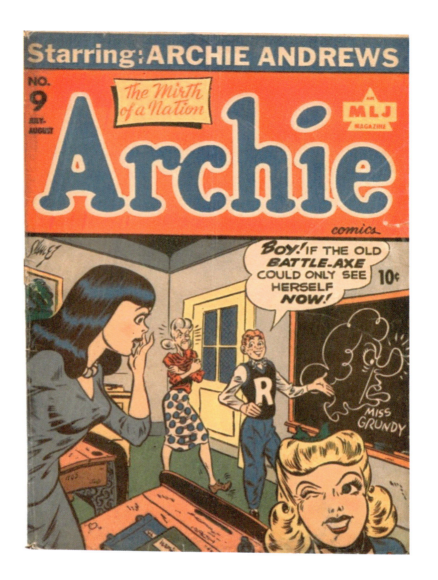

INDEX

Page 3   Events of the year UK
Page 17 Adverts in 1944
Page 24 Cost of living
Page 26 Births
Page 31 Deaths
Page 32 Sporting events
Page 35 Book Publications
Page 38 Movies
Page 49 Music
Page 56 World Events
Page 84 People in power

UK EVENTS OF 1944

January

1st Royal Air Force Mountain Rescue Service officially formed. The Royal Air Force Mountain Rescue Service (RAFMRS) provides the UK military's only all-weather search and rescue asset for the United Kingdom. Royal Air Force mountain rescue teams (MRTs) were first organised during World War II to rescue aircrew from the large number of aircraft crashes then occurring due to navigational errors in conjunction with bad weather and resulting poor visibility when flying in the vicinity of high ground. The practice at the time was to organise ad-hoc rescue parties from station medical sections and other ground personnel.

4th Benjamin Britten and Peter Pears begin a long association with Decca Records, recording four of Britten's folk song arrangements. Britten spends most of this year at the Old Mill in Snape, Suffolk, working on the opera Peter Grimes.

6th Britain and the U.S. announced that a jet-propelled aircraft would soon be in production.

8th German submarine U-757 was depth charged and sunk in the North Atlantic by the British destroyer Bayntun and the Canadian corvette Camrose.

10th British troops took Maungdaw in western Burma.

11th The Alfred Hitchcock-directed drama thriller film Lifeboat starring Talullah Bankhead and William Bendix was released.

12th Winston Churchill and Charles de Gaulle began a two-day conference in Marrakesh, Morocco centred on the co-operation of a French expeditionary force in the Allied invasion of Europe and the administration of France after the invasion.

17th A diplomatic incident occurred when The Soviet newspaper Pravda published a report claiming that representatives of Britain and Germany had met somewhere on the Iberian Peninsula to discuss making a separate peace. The British Foreign Office swiftly denied the rumour in an official message sent to the Soviet government.

18th The British 5th and 56th Divisions established themselves on the north bank of the Garigliano.

19th British bombers conducted their heaviest raid on Berlin yet, dropping 2,300 tons of bombs in just over half an hour.

20th Winston Churchill met with representatives of the Polish government-in-exile in an effort to break the diplomatic impasse with the Soviets. Churchill pressed the Poles to accept the Curzon Line as a basis for discussion, explaining that the Soviets' need for security as well as their enormous battlefield sacrifices to liberate Poland from the Germans entitled them to ask for revision of Polish frontiers. Churchill promised in return to challenge Moscow's demand for changes in the Polish government.

23rd The British destroyer Janus was sunk off Anzio by a Fritz X glide bomb.

24th The British hospital ship St David was bombed and sunk off Anzio despite being well-marked and lit in accordance with laws of war. 96 perished of the 229 aboard.

January

28th — A British telegram to Joseph Stalin warned that "the creation in Warsaw of another government other than that now recognized, as well as disturbances in Poland, would confront Great Britain and the United States with a problem, which would preclude agreement among the great powers."

29th — The British cruiser Spartan was sunk off Anzio by a Henschel Hs 293 glide bomb.

30th — British destroyer Hardy was crippled in the Arctic Sea by a torpedo from German submarine U-278 and had to be scrapped.

February

1st — Clothing restrictions were ended in Britain after two years, lifting unpopular limitations on the number of buttons, pockets and pleats on clothes.

9th — Bishop of Chichester George Bell started a debate in the House of Lords over the morality of the bombing of European cities when he made a speech questioning the practice. "I recognize the legitimacy of concentrated attack on industrial and military objectives, on airfields and air bases, in view especially of the coming of the Second Front," the Bishop said. "I fully realize that in attacks on centres of war industry and transport the killing of civilians when it is the result of bona-fide military activity is inevitable. But there must be a fair balance between the means employed and the purpose achieved. To obliterate a whole town because certain portions contain military and industrial establishments is to reject the balance ... How can there be discrimination in such matters when civilians, monuments, military objectives and industrial objectives all together form the target? How can the bombers aim at anything more than a great space when they see nothing and the bombing is blind?"

10th — German submarine U-545 was scuttled after being depth charged and crippled west of the Hebrides by a Vickers Wellington of No. 612 Squadron RAF.

PAYE (pay as you earn) system of tax collection introduced.

February

11th   At the Anzio beachhead, German forces captured "The Factory" from the British 1st Division.

12th   The British troop ship Khedive Ismail was torpedoed and sunk in the Indian Ocean with the loss of 1,297 people by Japanese submarine I-27, which was then sunk by British warships.

14th   In one of the few naval engagements in the Asian and Pacific theatre to involve German and Italian forces, the British submarine Tally-Ho sank the German-commanded U-boat UIT-23 (formerly the Italian submarine Giuliani).

16th   Lord Chancellor John Simon appeared before the House of Lords and made a speech defending the British bombing campaign. Referring specifically to the monastery at Monte Cassino, he said that most of the buildings there dated from the nineteenth century and that the most valuable art treasures and manuscripts had been moved elsewhere weeks and months earlier.

18th   The British cruiser Penelope was sunk off Naples by German submarine U-410 during the Battle of Anzio.

19th   187 planes of the Luftwaffe bombed London as part of Operation Steinbock. It was the heaviest bombing of the British capital since May 1941.

20th   The destroyer HMS Warwick (1917) is torpedoed by German submarine U-413 off Trevose Head, Cornwall, sinking in 6 minutes with the loss of 66 men, over half her crew.

21st   Churchill advised Stalin that the Polish government-in-exile was ready to accept the Curzon Line as a basis for talks and assured him that by the time they resumed diplomatic relations with the Soviets, their government would only consist of members willing to co-operate with Moscow. Stalin remained unconvinced.

22nd   Churchill gave a speech in the House of Commons aimed at dispelling Soviet distrust. Churchill said he supported the Soviet border demands in Poland as reasonable and stated that Britain had never guaranteed any Polish border.

25th   Queen Wilhelmina of the Netherlands narrowly escaped death when her London home was destroyed by German bombing.

26th   The Polish government-in-exile defied the British government's wishes and rejected the recognition of the Curzon Line as Poland's eastern frontier.

March

3rd   Joseph Stalin rejected British proposals to negotiate over the Polish-Soviet border.

4th   German submarine U-472 was sunk in the Barents Sea by Fairey Swordfish of 816 Naval Air Squadron.

8th   The British government announced plans to build 300,000 houses after the war.

10th   Ireland rejected a U.S. request to expel Axis diplomats from the country.

March

11th British forces took Buthidaung in Burma.

13th The British Government prohibits all travel between Great Britain and Ireland.

14th Winston Churchill told the House of Commons that the Allies intended to completely isolate Ireland to prevent military secrets leaking to the Axis, hinting that the border with Northern Ireland would soon be closed.

30 RAF planes were sent to attack Düsseldorf overnight.

15th German submarine U-653 was depth charged and sunk in the North Atlantic by British sloops Starling and Wild Goose.

HMS Starling   **HMS Wild Goose**

16th German submarine U-392 was sunk in the Strait of Gibraltar by American aircraft and British warships.

19th Michael Tippett's A Child of Our Time receives its first performances at London's Adelphi Theatre.

24th RAF Flight Sergeant Nicholas Alkemade survived a fall of 18,000 feet without a parachute when his Lancaster bomber was shot down east of Schmallenberg. Pine trees and soft snow broke his fall.

The "Great Escape" took place over the night of the 24th/25th, when 76 Royal Air Force prisoners of war escaped from Stalag Luft III in Lower Silesia.

27th The British merchant ship Tulagi was sunk in the Indian Ocean by German submarine U-532.

28th British MPs voted to give women teachers the same pay as men.

The British submarine Syrtis was lost in the Norwegian Sea, probably sunk by a naval mine.

29th German submarine U-961 was depth charged and sunk north of the Faroe Islands by the Royal Navy sloop HMS Starling.

30th The RAF suffered its worst loss of the war in a raid on Nuremberg. 96 of 795 aircraft were shot down, and cloud over the city meant that only a small proportion of the force hit their target.

April

1st — The British government banned visitors from going within ten miles of the coast between Land's End and the Wash.

2nd — The American Broadcasting Station in Europe (ABSIE) is established, transmitting from Britain in English, German, French, Dutch, Danish, and Norwegian to resistance movements in mainland Europe.

3rd — The Royal Navy carried out Operation Tungsten, an attack on the German battleship Tirpitz anchored in northern Norway. Fifteen bombs hit the battleship but the damage inflicted was not sufficient to sink or disable the target.

4th — Charlie Chaplin was acquitted by a federal court in Los Angeles of violating the Mann Act.

7th — Montagu Stopford's British XXXIII Corps was encircled by the Japanese near Jotsama, Burma.

8th — German submarine U-962 was depth charged and sunk northwest of Cape Finisterre by British warships.

10th — The RAF dropped a record 3,600 tons of bombs in a single raid on Germany, France and Belgium.

14th — The Japanese roadblock to the west of Kohima was broken and the encircled British XXXIII Corps was relieved after a week.

16th — The RAF made air raids on Romania for the first time, from bases in Italy.

19th — British launched Operation Cockpit - an air raid on Japanese-held Sabang, Indonesia, incurring heavy damage to the port facilities and airfield.

20th — The RAF set a new record for a single air raid, dropping 4,500 tons of bombs for Hitler's 55th birthday.

24th — An RAF raid reached Munich by encroaching on Swiss air space, thereby side-tracking the German air warning system.

25th — On Budget Day in the United Kingdom, Chancellor of the Exchequer Sir John Anderson announced that the deficit for the past year was £2.76 billion. This was £89 million smaller than the deficit forecast by Anderson's predecessor, the late Kingsley Wood, because government revenue was higher than expected. Anderson presented a budget with only minor changes from the previous year and no additional taxation.

27th — The British government banned all travel abroad.

28th — The first practice assault in Exercise Tiger, a series of large-scale rehearsals for D-Day, was held on Slapton Sands in Devon. The exercise was attacked by nine German E-boats that killed a total of 749 American servicemen. Two landing ships were sunk including USS LST-507.

30th — The first of 500,000 prefabricated homes went on show in London. In the United Kingdom, more than 156,000 prefabricated homes were built between 1945 and 1948.

May

2nd — German submarine U-674 was sunk in the Arctic Ocean north of Tromsø by a Fairey Swordfish aircraft of 842 Naval Air Squadron.

3rd — Exercise Fabius, the last major Allied rehearsals for the Normandy landings, take place along the south coast of England.

5th — The British Fourteenth Army counterattacked during the Battle of Imphal.

6th — British authorities announced that Mahatma Gandhi had been unconditionally released from custody on medical grounds after being interned at Aga Khan III's palace at Pune since August 1942.

10th — U.S. and British forces carried out Operation Diadem in Italy, breaking through German defences in the Liri Valley.

13th — Near Cassino, Italy, British Captain Richard Wakeford killed a number of the enemy and took 20 prisoners while armed with only a revolver. The following day he organized and led a force to attack a hill despite taking wounds to his face, arms and legs. Wakeford would be awarded the Victoria Cross for his actions.

15th — The first of three days of British Commando reconnaissance raids known as Operation Tarbrush began in northern France.

21st — German submarine U-453 was depth charged and sunk in the Ionian Sea by British warships.

24th — German submarine U-675 was depth charged and sunk off Ålesund by a Short Sunderland patrol bomber of No. 4 Squadron RAF.

25th — German submarine U-990 was depth charged and sunk in the North Sea by a B-24 Liberator of No. 59 Squadron RAF.

26th — Allied forces continued to advance toward Rome as American troops took Cori, the Canadians captured San Giovanni and the British took Monte Cairo.

30th — The British Eighth Army took Arce.

31st — German submarine U-289 was depth charged and sunk in the Barents Sea by British destroyer HMS Milne.

June

1st The BBC broadcast a coded message based on the Paul Verlaine poem Chanson d'automne to inform the French Resistance that the invasion of France was imminent. The Germans understood the intent of the message but failed to bring up sufficient forces.

2nd The Soham rail disaster occurred in the small town of Soham, Cambridgeshire, England when the cargo of an ammunition train exploded and killed two people.

5th World War II: final preparations for the Normandy landings take place in the south of England. Group Captain James Stagg correctly forecasts a brief improvement in weather conditions over the English Channel which will permit the following day's landings to take place (having been deferred from today due to unfavourable weather). The BBC transmits coded messages (including the second line of a poem by Paul Verlaine) to underground resistance fighters in France warning that the invasion of Europe is about to begin.

6th Winston Churchill announced the Normandy landings in an address to the House of Commons. "I cannot, of course, commit myself to any particular details," Churchill said. "Reports are coming in in rapid succession. So far the Commanders who are engaged report that everything is proceeding according to plan. And what a plan! This vast operation is undoubtedly the most complicated and difficult that has ever occurred ... Nothing that equipment, science or forethought could do has been neglected, and the whole process of opening this great new front will be pursued with the utmost resolution both by the commanders and by the United States and British Governments whom they serve."

7th The British began Operation Perch, an attempt to encircle and capture the city of Caen.

8th A B-24 of No. 224 Squadron RAF sank German submarine U-373 in the Bay of Biscay and then sank U-441 only some 20 minutes later in the English Channel.

12th U.S. and British forces in Normandy linked up near Carentan, forming a solid 50-mile (80 km) battlefront with 326,000 men and 54,000 vehicles.

13th RAF Bomber Command sent 221 aircraft to bomb Le Havre in its first daylight raid since May 1943. Three torpedo boats, fifteen S-boats, nine minesweepers and eight patrol boats were among the many German ships sunk in the raid.

June

14th — An RAF Mosquito recorded the first successful shooting down of a V-1 flying bomb over the English Channel.

17th — The Battle of Douvres Radar Station was fought. British 41 Commando, Royal Marines secured the surrender of a German garrison at Douvres-la-Délivrande.

18th — A V-1 flying bomb hit the Guards Chapel of Wellington Barracks during Sunday service and killed 121 people.

21st — The British destroyer Fury struck a mine off Sword Beach, Normandy and was declared a total loss.

24th — The British cargo ship Derrycunihy was sunk off Normandy with great loss of life by a Luftwaffe acoustic mine.

26th — British forces began Operation Epsom, again trying to take the German-occupied city of Caen.

July

2nd — The Razor's Edge by W. Somerset Maugham topped the New York Times Fiction Best Sellers list.

4th — No. 617 Squadron RAF attacked V-1 flying bomb facilities in a large cave at Saint-Leu-d'Esserent north of Paris.

6th — Winston Churchill gave a speech in the House of Commons about the V-1 campaign, revealing government figures that 2,752 had been killed and 8,000 injured by the flying bombs.

8th — British and Canadian forces launched Operation Charnwood with the goal of at least partially capturing the city of Caen, which remained in German hands despite repeated attempts to take it over the past month.

10th — Because of the danger of the German flying bombs, over 41,000 mothers and children left London in the second wartime exodus from the city and returned to their former wartime billets in the country.

15th — German submarine U-319 was depth charged and sunk in the North Sea by a B-24 of No. 206 Squadron RAF.

July

15th | Park Street riot in Bristol, a confrontation between black G.I.s and U.S. Military Police.

17th | The British government announced plans to build between 3 and 4 million houses in the decade following the end of the war.

20th | British destroyer Isis struck a mine and sank off Normandy.

24th | A British air raid at Kiel damaged the German submarine U-239, which never returned to active service.

25th | Operation Gaff: Six British commandos parachuted into German-occupied Orléans, France with the aim of killing or kidnapping German field marshal Erwin Rommel. When they learned that Rommel had already been injured they moved toward advancing U.S. Army lines on foot.

27th | The Gloster Meteor, the first British jet fighter and the Allies' only operational jet aircraft of the war, entered active service with No. 616 Squadron RAF.

30th | During the Battle of Normandy, the British Army began Operation Bluecoat with the goal of capturing Vire and Mont Pinçon.

August

1st | Scientists in the United Kingdom said that DDT had been found to act as an anti-malarial insecticide. Dichlorodiphenyltrichloroethane, commonly known as DDT, is a colourless, tasteless, and almost odourless crystalline chemical compound. DDT was used in the second half of World War II to limit the spread of the insect-borne diseases malaria and typhus among civilians and troops.

2nd | The Germans launched 316 V-1 flying bombs at London, the highest single-day total yet. Over 100 reached the capital, hitting Tower Bridge and doing great damage to the armament factories on the outskirts.

3rd | The British destroyer Quorn was sunk off Normandy during a heavy attack by German ships and aircraft.

8th | The Damasta sabotage occurred near the Cretan village of Damasta. Greek resistance fighters led by British Special Operations Executive Officer W. Stanley Moss attacked Axis occupation forces and killed 35 Germans and 10 Italians.

August

12th | A Special Air Service mission codenamed Operation Loyton began in the Vosges department of France. In the opening phase, a small advance party parachuted into the Vosges Mountains with the objective of contacting the local French Resistance and conducting a reconnaissance of the area.

World War II: The V-1 flying bomb campaign against London by the Germans reaches its 60th day, with more than 6,000 deaths, 17,000 injuries and damage or destruction to around 1 million buildings.

20th | American Liberty ship SS Richard Montgomery is wrecked off the Nore in the Thames Estuary with around 1,400 tonnes of explosives on board, never recovered.

21st | The British comedy-drama film A Canterbury Tale starring Eric Portman, Sheila Sim and Dennis Price premiered in the United Kingdom.

23rd | Freckleton air disaster: A USAAF Consolidated B-24 Liberator heavy bomber crashes into the village school at Freckleton, Lancashire, in a storm with 58 ground fatalities and 3 aircrew killed.

25th | British Commandos carried out Operation Rumford, an overnight raid on the French Île d'Yeu. When they got there, they discovered the Germans had already withdrawn.

28th | The BBC began broadcasting in Dutch to Indonesia and in French to southeast Asia.

31st | King George VI made Bernard Montgomery a field marshal.

September

3rd | The British Second Army captured Brussels while the U.S. First Army took Tournai.

September

4th The British Guards Armoured Division took Kortenberg and Leuven.

6th The British government relaxed blackout restrictions and suspended compulsory training for the Home Guard.

7th The Belgian government leaves the UK and returns to Belgium following the liberation of Brussels on 3rd September.

8th The first V-2 rocket attack on London takes place, striking in the Chiswick district of the city and resulting in the deaths of three people. The British government did not acknowledge the new German weapon until November.

10th RAF Bomber Command began Operation Paravane, another attack on the German battleship Tirpitz anchored in northern Norway.

14th Canadian and British troops pushing through the Gothic Line captured Coriano.

17th Blackout restrictions were relaxed in London.

18th The Japanese hell ship Jun'yō Maru was sunk off Sumatra by the British submarine Tradewind with the loss of 5,620 lives, the worst maritime disaster in history up to that time.

23rd An RAF bombing raid destroyed an aqueduct on the Dortmund-Ems Canal and brought a halt to the shipment of prefabricated U-boat parts via this route.

24th British troops captured Deurne, Netherlands.

25th V-2 rockets aimed at Ipswich and Norwich by the Germans miss their targets by a distance.

26th The British Eighth Army in Italy crossed the Rubicon.

27th The British destroyer Rockingham (formerly the USS Swasey) struck a mine in the North Sea and sank under tow.

28th Winston Churchill made a speech in the House of Commons reviewing the progress of the war and announcing that a Jewish brigade would be formed to take part in active operations. "I know there is a vast number of Jews serving with our forces and the American forces throughout all the armies, but it seems to me indeed appropriate that a special Jewish unit of that race which has suffered indescribable torment from the Nazis should be represented as a distinct formation among the forces gathered for their final overthrow," Churchill explained. "I have no doubt that they will not only take part in the struggle but also in the occupation which will follow."

October

4th German submarines U-92, U-228 and U-437 were all sunk or rendered inoperable by an air raid on Bergen by RAF aircraft.

5th Five pilots of No. 401 Squadron RCAF participated in the shooting down of a Messerschmitt Me 262 over the Netherlands, marking the first time that a jet fighter had been shot down by enemy fire.

October

8th   Sir William Jowitt was appointed Britain's first Minister of National Insurance.

9th   The Fourth Moscow Conference began. Winston Churchill, Joseph Stalin and U.S. ambassador W. Averell Harriman met to discuss the future of Europe.

12th   The British destroyer Loyal struck a mine in the Tyrrhenian Sea and was rendered a constructive total loss.

18th   The British Eighth Army in Italy captured Galeata.

29th   RAF Bomber Command carried out Operation Obviate aimed at sinking the German battleship Tirpitz at Tromsø. The attack was foiled by cloud cover and the bombs caused only minor damage.

30th   The British Eighth Army reached Forlì. The Allied advance in Italy had slowed considerably in recent days and time was running out to realize the objective of taking Bologna before winter.

31st   25 British Mosquito planes carried out the successful Aarhus Air Raid targeting the Gestapo headquarters at Aarhus University in Denmark.

November

1st   A naval battle was fought in the Kvarner Gulf off Croatia between a Royal Navy destroyer flotilla and a Kriegsmarine force of two corvettes and a destroyer. The result was a British victory as all three German ships were sunk.

4th   RAF Bomber Command sent 749 aircraft to conduct the last major raid on Bochum. Over 4,000 buildings were destroyed and nearly 1,000 people were killed.

5th   British troops in Italy captured Ravenna, cutting the railway line to Bologna.

6th   In Liverpool, the largest penicillin factory in the world began production.

8th   Joseph Goebbels announced the V-2 rocket campaign for the first time. Winston Churchill followed suit and finally announced that England had been under rocket attack, providing the people of London with an explanation for all the mysterious explosions of recent weeks.

11th   German submarine U-1200 was depth charged and sunk south of Ireland by British warships.

12th   RAF Bomber Command carried out Operation Catechism and, after trying unsuccessfully for months, finally sank the German battleship Tirpitz near Tromsø.

13th   Civil air service returned to London for the first time since September 1939.

17th   The British Second Army captured Wessem.

20th   English author P. G. Wodehouse, who had made broadcasts over enemy radio in France during the Nazi occupation, was arrested in Paris.

November

22nd	The British submarine Stratagem was depth charged and sunk in the Strait of Malacca by the Japanese submarine chaser CH 35.
25th	A German V-2 rocket struck the intersection of High Holborn and Chancery Lane in the Holborn section of London, killing 6 and wounding 292. Then, in the worst V-2 attack of the war, another one landed across the street from the Woolworths department store in New Cross, South London and killed 168.
27th	RAF Fauld explosion: A military accident occurred at the RAF Fauld underground munitions storage depot east of Hanbury, Staffordshire, killing about 70 people.
30th	A German V-2 rocket struck Shooter's Hill in South East London at 1:00 a.m., killing 23.

December

3rd	The British Home Guard formally stood down. The Home Guard (initially Local Defence Volunteers or LDV) was an armed citizen militia supporting the British Army during the Second World War. Operational from 1940 to 1944, the Home Guard had 1.5 million local volunteers otherwise ineligible for military service, such as those who were too young or too old to join the regular armed services (regular military service was restricted to those aged 18 to 41) and those in reserved occupations.

5th	British forces in Greece shelled communist positions near Piraeus.
6th	In Britain the official process of returning evacuees began in regions unaffected by the V-weapon attacks.
9th	German submarine U-387 was depth charged and sunk in the Barents Sea by the Royal Navy corvette Bamborough Castle.
11th	The British Eighth Army in Italy crossed the Lamone.
12th	British General Harold Alexander was promoted to field marshal and made Supreme Commander of Allied Force Headquarters in the Mediterranean.
13th	German submarine U-365 was depth charged and sunk in the Arctic Ocean by Fairey Swordfish aircraft of 813 Naval Air Squadron.

December

14th	The British escort destroyer Aldenham was sunk by a naval mine in the Adriatic Sea off Pag. Aldenham was the last Royal Navy destroyer lost in World War II.
17th	German submarine U-772 was depth charged and sunk south of Cork, Ireland by Royal Navy frigate Nyasaland.
18th	British troops in Greece began an offensive against the ELAS rebels.
19th	Council of Industrial Design established. Founded by Hugh Dalton, President of the Board of Trade in the wartime Government. Its objective was 'to promote by all practicable means the improvement of design in the products of British industry'.
20th	British General Ronald Scobie warned Greek civilians to stay out of areas occupied by ELAS forces because they may be subjected to bombing raids.
24th	Fifty German V-1 flying bombs, air-launched from Heinkel He 111 bombers flying over the North Sea, targeted Manchester in England, killing 42 and injuring more than 100 in the Oldham area.
25th	Winston Churchill arrived in Athens to try to stop the fighting.
26th	German submarine U-486 torpedoed the British frigates Affleck and Capel in the English Channel off Cherbourg. Affleck was declared a constructive total loss and Capel was sunk.
27th	David Lloyd George announced his retirement from British Parliament.
29th	British Commandos carried out Operation Partridge over the night of December 29/30, a diversionary raid behind German lines in Italy.
31st	Twelve de Havilland Mosquitos of the RAF bombed Oslo, Norway, targeting a Gestapo headquarters in the city. The RAF initially believed the raid was successful, but the target building was in fact undamaged and other civilian buildings were hit instead. 78 Norwegians and 28 Germans were killed in the worst single incident in Oslo during the war.

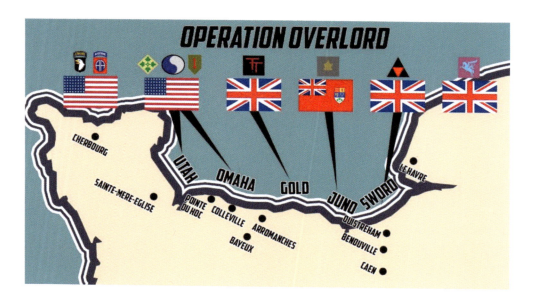

ADVERTS OF 1944

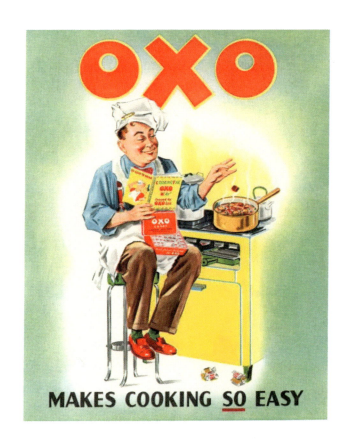

NOW YOU EVEN PLANT WITH A TUBE

★The "Fluora Seedasets" people have invented a useful little gadget that enables seedlings to be grown individually. They've done away with all that thinning out process and wastage of seed. We're not here to advertise this new gadget (although we don't mind passing on a good tip when we hear of one), our main object is to point out that our old friend the steel tube is the basis of this invention. Maybe by continually pointing out the universal usefulness of steel tubes we may plant a seed or two ourselves among manufacturers with fertile minds.

★ If you want a green thumb, don't write us— Write: Fluora Seedasets, Merrilees, Grove Lane, Chalfont St. Peter, Bucks.

An advertisement for
BRITANNIA TUBE CO · LTD
Glover St., Birmingham
BY TUBE INVESTMENTS LTD

TO THOSE RESPONSIBLE FOR THE HEALTH OF MEN LIKE THIS

Thousands of working hours are lost through sickness absenteeism. Colds, flu, bronchitis, as well as sepsis following neglected cuts and minor injuries, deplete our man power. This wastage can be reduced by a practical system that can be put into operation now.

Write to Newton, Chambers & Co. Ltd., Thorncliffe, Sheffield, for details of this practical method, the Izal System of Industrial Hygiene, which has been tested and proved, and is in operation in hundreds of factories.

THE IZAL SYSTEM OF INDUSTRIAL HYGIENE

Thanks to...

1865 – 1943

The family will appreciate that little addition of LEMCO BEEF EXTRACT. It makes all the difference to your cooking.

LEMCO THE ORIGINAL
Concentrated Beef Extract

☞ One pound of LEMCO contains the concentrated juices of over 30 pounds of prime beef.

— PREPARED BY OXO LIMITED, LONDON —

WILLS'S
THREE CASTLES
CIGARETTES

20 for 2'8

One expects to pay a little more for a cigarette of such excellent Quality.

Issued by The Imperial Tobacco Company (of Great Britain and Ireland), Ltd.

"WE'LL SAY IT'S WORTH BARKING FOR!"

Dogs of all breeds love and thrive on "Chappie". This makes it all the more embarrassing for us to warn you that this complete food is in short supply and that its sale, in all fairness, is restricted to old customers.

"Chappie" is the complete, scientifically balanced, all-round diet for dogs. Vets, breeders and other experts agree that it provides the essential nourishment for the promotion of robust health. If your dog is deprived of "Chappie," just tell him how sorry we are. Give him this message from his more fortunate brothers: "Cheer up, old chap, we know the good things you are missing. Bark for the downfall of Hitler. Then, when peace comes, see that your master puts you on 'Chappie'. We'll say it's worth barking for!"

SAVE BONES FOR SALVAGE

BONES—even those your dog has done with—are vital to the war effort. Salvage every scrap and put out for collection

In air-tight jars, 1/-.

"CHAPPIE" DOG FOOD

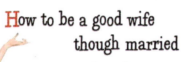

COST OF LIVING 1944

A conversion of pre-decimal to decimal money

The Pound, 1971 became the year of decimalization when the pound became 100 new pennies. Prior to that the pound was equivalent to 20 shillings. Money prior to 1971 was written £/s/d. (d being for pence). Below is a chart explaining the monetary value of each coin before and after 1971.

Symbol	Before 1971	After 1971
£	Pound (240 pennies)	Pound (100 new pennies)
s	Shilling (12 pennies)	5 pence
d	Penny	¼ of a penny
¼d	Farthing	1 penny
½d	Halfpenny	½ pence
3d	Threepence	About 1/80 of a pound
4d	Groat (four pennies)	
6d	Sixpence (Tanner)	2½ new pence
2s	Florin (2 shillings)	10 pence
2s/6d	Half a crown (2 shillings and 6 pence)	12½ pence
5s	Crown	25 pence
10s	10-shilling note (10 bob)	50 pence
10s/6d	½ Guinea	52½ pence
21s	1 Guinea	105 pence

Oatmeal	**3½d (1½p) per lb**
Meat (average price)	1/2 (6p) per lb
Potatoes	**7d (3p) per ½ stone (7lb)**
Sugar	4d (1½p) per lb
Milk	**9d (3½p) per quart**
Cheese	1/1 (5½p) per lb
Bacon	**1/10½ (9p) per lb**
Eggs large	2/- (10p) per dozen and small 1/9 (8½p) per dozen
Bread	**9d (3½p) per 4lb loaf.**

Strawberry plants 12 for 2/6 (12½p)
Raspberry canes 12 for 3/6 (17½p)
Darwin Tulip bulbs 12 for 7/6 (37½p)
100 mixed Daffodil, Tulip and Narcissus bulbs for 19/- (95p)

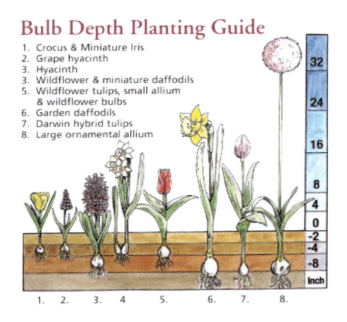

Cadbury's Red Label drinking chocolate 10d (4p) per ½lb
Bournville cocoa 9½d (3½p) per ½lb
Bourn-Vita 1/5 (7p) per ½lb

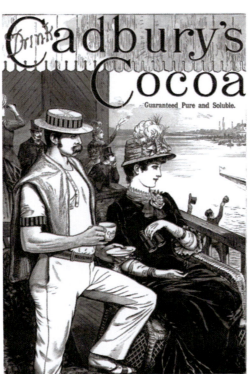

Woodwards Gripe Water 1/5 (7p) per bottle
Booth's Dry Gin £1/5/3 (£1.26) per bottle and 13/3 (66p) per ½ bottle
Wooden soled shoes (which were really clogs) 5 coupons and 12/4 (62p)
One-handed storm-proof cigarette lighter 6/6 (32½p) plus 6d (2½p) postage and packing.

BRITISH BIRTHS

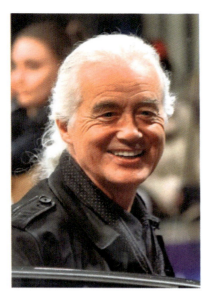

James Patrick Page OBE born 9th January 1944 and is an English musician who achieved international success as the guitarist and founder of the rock band Led Zeppelin. Page began his career as a studio session musician in London and, by the mid-1960s, alongside Big Jim Sullivan, was one of the most sought-after session guitarists in Britain. He was a member of the Yardbirds from 1966 to 1968. When the Yardbirds broke up, he founded Led Zeppelin, which was active from 1968 to 1980. Page is widely considered to be one of the greatest and most influential guitarists of all time. Rolling Stone magazine has described Page as "the pontiff of power riffing" and ranked him number three in their 2015 list of the "100 Greatest Guitarists of All Time", behind Jimi Hendrix and Eric Clapton. In 2010, he was ranked number two in Gibson's list of "Top 50 Guitarists of All Time" and, in 2007, number four on Classic Rock's "100 Wildest Guitar Heroes". He was inducted into the Rock and Roll Hall of Fame twice: once as a member of the Yardbirds (1992) and once as a member of Led Zeppelin (1995).

Gerald Norman Springer born 13th February 1944 is a British-American broadcaster, journalist, actor, producer, former lawyer, and politician. Gerald Norman Springer was born in the London Underground station of Highgate while the station was in use as a shelter from German bombing during World War II. In January 1949, at the age of four, Springer emigrated with his parents to the United States, settling in the Kew Gardens neighbourhood of Queens, New York City. In 1970, Springer ran for Congress. He failed to unseat incumbent Republican Donald D. Clancy, but took 45% of the vote in a traditionally Republican district. In 2005, a UK version of the show aired on Britain's ITV network titled The Springer Show. A subdued and more tongue-in-cheek version of the U.S. show, it beat its talk-show rival Trisha Goddard five to one in the ratings. In 2022, Springer competed in season eight of The Masked Singer US as "Beetle". He was eliminated on "Muppet Night" alongside Kat Graham as "Robo-Girl".

Roger Harry Daltrey CBE born 1st March 1944 and is an English singer, musician and actor. He is a co-founder and the lead singer of the rock band The Who. The Who are considered one of the most influential rock bands of the 20th century and have sold over 100 million records worldwide. As a member of the band, Daltrey received a Lifetime achievement award from the British Phonographic Industry in 1988. He was inducted into the Rock and Roll Hall of Fame in 1990, and the UK Music Hall of Fame in 2005. He and Pete Townshend received Kennedy Centre Honours in 2008 and The George and Ira Gershwin Award for Lifetime Musical Achievement at UCLA on 21st May 2016. Daltrey has also been an actor and film producer, with roles in films, theatre, and television. Planet Rock listeners voted him rock's fifth-greatest voice in 2009 and he was ranked number 61 on Rolling Stone's list of the 100 greatest singers of all time in 2010.

Sir Ranulph Twisleton-Wykeham-Fiennes, 3rd Baronet OBE born 7th March 1944. He is a British explorer, writer and poet, who holds several endurance records. Fiennes served in the British Army for eight years, including a period on counter-insurgency service while attached to the Army of the Sultanate of Oman. He later undertook numerous expeditions and was the first person to visit both the North Pole and South Pole by surface means and the first to completely cross Antarctica on foot. In May 2009, at the age of 65, he climbed to the summit of Mount Everest. According to the Guinness Book of World Records in 1984 he was the world's greatest living explorer. Fiennes has written numerous books about his army service and his expeditions as well as books on explorers Robert Falcon Scott and Ernest Shackleton. Most recently Fiennes was an expert guest commentator on the PBS documentary Chasing Shackleton which aired in January 2014.

General Sir Michael David Jackson, GCB, CBE, DSO, DL born 21st March 1944 and is a retired British Army officer and one of its most high-profile generals since the Second World War. Originally commissioned into the Intelligence Corps in 1963, he transferred to the Parachute Regiment in 1970, with which he served two of his three tours of duty in Northern Ireland. In 1995–1996, Jackson served his first tour in the Balkans, where he commanded a multi-national division of the Implementation Force. Following a staff job in the UK, he was appointed commander of NATO's Allied Rapid Reaction Corps (ARRC) in 1997. He returned to the Balkans with the ARRC during the Kosovo War. Upon his return to the UK, Jackson was promoted to full general and appointed Commander-in-Chief, Land Command, the second-most senior position in the British Army. He was succeeded as CGS by General Sir Richard Dannatt in 2006, and retired from the Army after serving for almost 45 years. Jackson continues to speak on military matters and works as a consultant and guest lecturer.

Michael Fish, MBE FRMetS born 27th April 1944 in Eastbourne, Sussex is a British weather forecaster. From 1974 to 2004, he was a television presenter for BBC Weather. Michael Fish was the longest-serving broadcast meteorologist on British television. He joined the Met Office in 1962 and started on BBC Radio in 1971, moving to the role on television in 1974. A few hours before the Great Storm of 1987 broke, on 15 October 1987, he said during a forecast: "Earlier on today, apparently, a woman rang the BBC and said she heard there was a hurricane on the way. Well, if you're watching, don't worry, there isn't!". The storm was the worst to hit South East England for three centuries, causing record damage and killing 19 people. 15 years later he commented that if he were given a penny for every mention of that forecast, he would be a millionaire. In 2012, a clip of the bulletin was shown as part of a video montage in the London 2012 Summer Olympics opening ceremony. On 18th July 2022, Fish appeared live in the studio on BBC2s Newsnight.

John Robert "Joe" Cocker OBE 20th May 1944 and died 22nd December 2014. He was an English singer known for his gritty, bluesy voice and dynamic stage performances that featured expressive body movements. His first album featured a recording of the Beatles' "With a Little Help from My Friends", which brought him to near-instant stardom. The song reached number one in the UK in 1968, became a staple of his many live shows. He continued his success with his second album, which included a second Beatles song: "She Came in Through the Bathroom Window". Cocker's best-selling song was the U.S. number one "Up Where We Belong", a duet with Jennifer Warnes that earned a 1983 Grammy Award. He released a total of 22 studio albums over a 43-year recording career. In 1993, Cocker was nominated for the Brit Award for Best British Male. He was awarded a bronze Sheffield Legends plaque in his hometown in 2007, and received an OBE the following year for services to music.

Robert Powell born 1st June 1944 and is an English actor. His first film part was in Robbery (1967), which starred Stanley Baker and was about the Great Train Robbery, in which he played the second man or locomotive driver's assistant. He had a small role in the original film version of The Italian Job (1969) playing one of the gang but had to wait a few years for his first success, playing scientist Toby Wren in the BBC's science fiction series, Doomwatch in 1970. He then played Jesus of Nazareth in Jesus of Nazareth (1977) following a successful second audition with Franco Zeffirelli. In 1978, Powell took the leading role of Richard Hannay in the third film version of The Thirty-Nine Steps. In 2005 Powell began appearing in the BBC soap opera Holby City, as a hospital administrator. On Easter Sunday 1 April 2018, he appeared in a Smithsonian Channel Documentary Series based on his portrayal of the Franco Zeffirelli mini-series Jesus of Nazareth titled, The Real Jesus of Nazareth, narrated by Judd Hirsch.

Winifred Jacqueline Fraser Bisset born 13th September 1944 is a British actress. She began her film career in 1965 and first came to prominence in 1968 with roles in The Detective, Bullitt, and The Sweet Ride, for which she received a Golden Globe nomination as Most Promising Newcomer. In 1970, Bisset was one of the many stars in the disaster film Airport; her role was that of a pregnant stewardess carrying Dean Martin's love child. It was a huge hit at the box office, ushering in an era of disaster films. In 1984 Bisset made the wartime drama Forbidden with Jürgen Prochnow, and earned a CableACE Award nomination as Best Actress. In 1995, Bisset was nominated for a César Award for her role in the French film La Cérémonie, directed by Claude Chabrol. In 2010, Bisset was awarded the Legion of Honour insignia, with French President Nicolas Sarkozy calling her "a movie icon". In 2019, she co-starred with Fabio Testi in the Lifetime movie Very Valentine. In 2020, Bisset joined the cast of Birds of Paradise from Amazon Studios, shot in Budapest.

Graham Taylor OBE born 15th September 1944 and died 12th January 2017. He was an English football player, manager, pundit and chairman of Watford Football Club. He became a professional player, playing at full back for Grimsby Town and Lincoln City. He retired as a result of injury in 1972. He then became a manager and coach. He won the Fourth Division title with Lincoln in 1976, before moving to Watford in 1977. He took Watford from the Fourth Division to the First in five years. Under Taylor, Watford were First Division runners-up in 1982–83, and FA Cup finalists in 1984. Taylor took over at Aston Villa in 1987, leading the club to promotion in 1988 and 2nd place in the First Division in 1989–90. In July 1990, he became the manager of the England team. They qualified for the 1992 European Championship, but were knocked out in the group stages. Taylor resigned in November 1993, after the team failed to qualify for the 1994 FIFA World Cup in the United States. Taylor returned to club management in March 1994 with Wolverhampton Wanderers.

Anne Josephine Robinson born 26th September 1944 is an English television presenter and journalist. Her father was a schoolteacher. Her mother, Anne Josephine (née Wilson) was an agricultural businesswoman from Northern Ireland, where she was the manager of a market stall. When she came to England, she married into her husband's family of wholesale chicken dealers, and sold rationed rabbit following the Second World War. She inherited the family market stall in Liverpool and transformed it into one of the largest wholesale poultry businesses in the north of England. On leaving school, Anne chose journalism over training for the theatre. Anne returned to Fleet Street in 1980, working as columnist and assistant editor of the Daily Mirror. From 1986, she began sitting in on television viewers' show Points of View for regular presenter Barry Took, taking over from Took permanently in 1988. In the UK, Robinson is best known for hosting the game show The Weakest Link. In February 2021, Robinson was announced as the next host of the game show Countdown.

John Alec Entwistle born 9th October 1944 and died 27th June 2002. He was an English musician who was the bassist for the rock band The Who. His musical career began aged 7, when he started taking piano lessons. He met Pete Townshend in the second year of school, and the two formed a trad jazz band, the Confederates. Entwistle, in particular, was having difficulty hearing his trumpet with rock bands, and decided to switch to playing guitar, but due to his large fingers, and also his fondness for the low guitar tones of Duane Eddy, he decided to take up the bass guitar instead. Daltrey was aware of Entwistle from school, and asked him to join as a bass guitarist for his band, the Detours. Entwistle was known for being the quietest member of the Who, he in fact often exerted major influences on the rest of the band. For instance, Entwistle was the first member of the band to wear a Union Jack waistcoat. Entwistle died in Room 658 at the Hard Rock Hotel and Casino in Paradise, Nevada.

William David Trimble, Baron Trimble, PC born 15th October 1944 and passed away 25th July 2022. He was a British politician who was the first First Minister of Northern Ireland from 1998 to 2002, and leader of the Ulster Unionist Party (UUP) from 1995 to 2005. Trimble began his career teaching law at The Queen's University of Belfast in the 1970s, during which time he began to get involved with the paramilitary-linked Vanguard Progressive Unionist Party (VPUP). He was elected to the Northern Ireland Constitutional Convention in 1975, and joined the UUP in 1978 after the VPUP disbanded. In 1995 he was unexpectedly elected as the leader of the UUP. He was instrumental in the negotiations that led to the Good Friday Agreement in 1998 and won the Nobel Peace Prize that year for his efforts. He was later elected to become the first First Minister of Northern Ireland, although his tenure was turbulent and frequently interrupted by disagreements over the timetable for Provisional Irish Republican Army decommissioning.

Sir Timothy Miles Bindon Rice born 10th November 1944 and is an English lyricist and author. Rice was educated at three independent schools: Aldwickbury School in Hertfordshire, St Albans School and Lancing College. He left Lancing with GCE A-Levels in History and French and then started work as an articled clerk for a law firm in London, having decided not to apply for a university place. Rice joined EMI Records as a management trainee in 1966. When EMI producer Norrie Paramor left to set up his own organization in 1968, Rice joined him as an assistant producer, working with, among others, Cliff Richard and The Scaffold. Rice became famous for his collaborations with Andrew Lloyd Webber, with whom he wrote Joseph and the Amazing Technicolor Dreamcoat, Jesus Christ Superstar, Evita and additional songs for the 2011 West End production of The Wizard of Oz. He released his autobiography Oh What a Circus: The Autobiography of Tim Rice in 1998, which covered his childhood and early adult life until the opening of the original London production of Evita in 1978.

Jonathan King born Kenneth George King, 6th December 1944 and is an English singer, songwriter and record producer. As an independent producer, he discovered and named the rock band Genesis in 1967, producing their first album From Genesis to Revelation. He founded his own label UK Records in 1972. He released and produced songs for 10cc and the Bay City Rollers. While living in New York in the 1980s, King appeared on radio and television in the UK, including on the BBC's Top of the Pops and Entertainment USA. In the early 1990s he produced the Brit Awards, and from 1995 he selected and produced the British entries for the Eurovision Song Contest, including the winning entry in 1997, "Love Shine a Light" by Katrina and the Waves. In September 2001, King was convicted of child sexual abuse and sentenced to seven years in prison for having sexually assaulted five boys, aged 14 and 15, in the 1980s. In November 2001, he was acquitted of 22 similar charges. He was released on parole in March 2005.

DEATHS

Commander Harold Godfrey Lowe RD, RNR born 21st November 1882 and died 12th May 1944. He was the fifth officer of the RMS Titanic. He was amongst the 3 officers to survive the disaster. At 14, he ran away from his home in Barmouth where he had attended school and joined the Merchant Navy, serving along the West African Coast. Lowe started as a ship's boy aboard the Welsh coastal schooners as he worked to attain his certifications. By the time he started with the White Star Line, in 1911, he had gained his Master's certificate and, in his own words, "experience with pretty well every ship afloat – the different classes of ships afloat – from the schooner to the square-rigged sailing vessel, and from that to steamships, and of all sizes." Lowe reported to White Star's Liverpool offices at nine o'clock in the morning on 26th March 1912, and travelled to board Titanic at Belfast the following day. Lowe died of hypertension on 12 May 1944 at the age of 61. His body was buried at Llandrillo-yn-Rhos churchyard in Rhos-on-Sea in North Wales.

Éliane Sophie Plewman born 6th December 1917 and died 13th September 1944. She was a British agent of Special Operations Executive (SOE) and member of the French Resistance working as a courier for the "MONK circuit" in occupied France during World War II. SOE's objective was to conduct espionage, sabotage and reconnaissance against the Axis Powers, especially Nazi Germany in occupied Europe and to aid local resistance movements. Plewman was captured by the Gestapo, and later executed by the SS in Dachau. After the outbreak of the Second World War in 1939, Plewman worked for the Press Section of the British Embassies in Madrid and Lisbon until 1941. In 1942, she returned to Britain to work for the Spanish Press section of the Ministry of Information. Between 0800 and 1000 hours the next morning, 13 September 1944, Plewman and three other SOE agents were taken from their cell and forced to kneel in pairs before being executed by a single shot to the head by executioner Wilhelm Ruppert.

Air Chief Marshal Sir Trafford Leigh-Mallory, KCB, DSO & Bar born 11th July 1892 and died 14th November 1944. He was a senior commander in the Royal Air Force. Leigh-Mallory served as a Royal Flying Corps pilot and squadron commander during the First World War. Remaining in the newly formed RAF after the war, Leigh-Mallory served in a variety of staff and training appointments throughout the 1920s and 1930s. During the pre-Second World War build-up, he was Air Officer Commanding (AOC) No. 12 (Fighter) Group and shortly after the end of the Battle of Britain, took over command of No. 11 (Fighter) Group, defending the approach to London. In 1942 he became the Commander-in-Chief (C-in-C) of Fighter Command before being selected in 1943 to be the C-in-C of the Allied Expeditionary Air Force, which made him the air commander for the Allied Invasion of Normandy. He was one of the most senior British officers and the most senior RAF officer to be killed in the Second World War.

SPORTING EVENTS 1944

Due to World War II sporting events were hit hard in the United Kingdom

The 1944 Summer Olympics, which were to be officially known as the Games of the XIII Olympiad, were cancelled because of World War II. They would have been held in London, England, United Kingdom, which won the bid on the first ballot in a June 1939 IOC election over Rome, Detroit, Lausanne, Athens, Budapest, Helsinki and Montreal. The selection was made at the 38th IOC Session in London in 1939. Because of the cancellation, London went on to host the 1948 Summer Olympics.

In spite of the war, the IOC organised many events to celebrate the fiftieth anniversary of its foundation at its headquarters in Lausanne, Switzerland. Held from 17 to 19 June 1944, this celebration was referred to as "The Jubilee Celebrations of IOC" by Carl Diem, the originator of the modern tradition of the Olympic torch relay.

Polish Prisoners of War (POWs) in the Woldenberg (Dobiegniew) Oflag II-C POW camp were granted permission by their German captors to stage an unofficial POW Olympics during 23 July to 13 August 1944, and an Olympic Flag made with a bed sheet and pieces of coloured scarves was raised. The event has been considered to be a demonstration of the Olympic spirit transcending war.

The Olympic game we re-scheduled for London 1948.

Chess

27th June 1944 – Vera Manchik-Stevenson, first official Women's World Chess Champion (since 1927), represented Russia (1927), Czechoslovakia (1930–37), and England (1939), who was widowed the previous year, still holding the title, her younger sister, Olga Menchik-Rubery, and their mother were killed in a V-1 rocket bombing raid which destroyed their home at 47 Gauden Road in the Clapham area of South London. According to some sources, Kent was the place of their death.

Rugby League

The 1943–44 Northern Rugby Football Union season was the fifth season of the rugby league's 'Wartime Emergency League necessitated by the Second World War. As in the previous (fourth) Wartime season, the clubs each played a different number of games, but this season clubs re-joined the league and there were now 16 of the original clubs taking part in the Competition (but still only Oldham, St Helens and Wigan from west of the Pennines). At the completion of the regular season Wakefield Trinity were on top of the league on both points and percentage success (with 38 points from 22 games and a percentage success of 86.36%), and Wigan were second (34 points from 21 games @ 80.95%). As of 2017, this is the only occasion that Wakefield Trinity have finished top of the league.

No other sports we contested in Great Britain in 1944 other than horse racing.

Horse Racing 1944

The 2000 Guineas Stakes is a Group 1 flat horse race in Great Britain open to three-year-old thoroughbred colts and fillies. It is run on the Rowley Mile at Newmarket over a distance of 1 mile (1,609 metres), and it is scheduled to take place each year in late April or early May. It is one of Britain's five Classic races, and at present it is the first to be run in the year. It also serves as the opening leg of the Triple Crown, followed by the Derby and the St Leger, although the feat of winning all three has been rarely attempted in recent decades.

Garden Path was a British Thoroughbred racehorse and broodmare who won the classic 2000 Guineas in 1944. In a racing career conducted entirely at Newmarket Racecourse the filly ran six times and won three races. She was one of the best British two-year-olds of 1943, when she won one race and was placed in both the Middle Park Stakes and the Cheveley Park Stakes. After winning on her first appearance of 1944 she became the first (and still the only) filly since 1902 to win the 2000 Guineas against colts. On her only subsequent race she was injured when finishing unplaced in the Derby. She was retired from racing at the end of the season and had some success as a broodmare. Garden Path was retired to become a broodmare at her owner's stud. She produced five winners, three at stakes level.

The best of her offspring was Leading Light, a colt sired by Hyperion who won the Knights Royal Stakes. The race which would later become known as the Queen Elizabeth II Stakes.

The Derby Stakes, also known as the Epsom Derby or the Derby, and as the Cazoo Derby for sponsorship reasons, is a Group 1 flat horse race in England open to three-year-old colts and fillies. It is run at Epsom Downs Racecourse in Surrey on the first Saturday of June each year, over a distance of one mile, four furlongs and 6 yards (2,420 metres). It was first run in 1780. It is Britain's richest flat horse race, and the most prestigious of the five Classics. It is sometimes referred to as the "Blue Riband" of the turf.

Ocean Swell was a British Thoroughbred racehorse and sire. In a career that lasted from 1943 to 1945 he ran fifteen times and won six races. As a three-year-old 1944 he won the New Derby, a wartime substitute for The Derby run at Newmarket. Ocean Swell started a 28/1 outsider while Garden Path and Growing Confidence disputed favouritism in a field of twenty. The early pace was slow, but the field quickened just after half way and Nevett sent his horse into the lead just over three furlongs from the finish. In a "furious" finish, Ocean Swell stayed on strongly in the closing stages, showing "pluck and stamina" to win a "great fight" by a neck from Tehran, with the fast-finishing Happy Landing a short head back in third. He later developed into a specialist stayer, winning the Jockey Club Cup in the autumn of 1944 and the Gold Cup at the following summer. He was then retired to stud where he had limited success.

The St Leger Stakes is a Group 1 flat horse race in Great Britain open to three-year-old thoroughbred colts and fillies. It is run at Doncaster over a distance of 1 mile, 6 furlongs and 115 yards (2,921 metres), and it is scheduled to take place each year in September. Established in 1776, the St Leger is the oldest of Britain's five Classics. It is the last of the five to be run each year, and its distance is longer than any of the other four. The St Leger is the final leg of the English Triple Crown, which begins with the 2000 Guineas and continues with the Derby.

Tehran was a British Thoroughbred racehorse and sire, who raced during World War II and was best known for winning the classic St Leger in 1944. Doncaster Racecourse, the traditional home of the St Leger was unavailable for racing in 1944 and substitute "New St Leger" was run at Newmarket in September. Ridden by Gordon Richards, Tehran started at odds of 9/2 in a field of seventeen runners which also included Ocean Swell and the filly Hycilla, the winner of the Oaks Stakes, who started favourite. He won by one and a half lengths from Lord Derby's colt Borealis with Ocean Swell third. After the race Richards commented "I made the first forward move and was followed by Harry Wragg on Borealis. Harry must have got almost to Tehran's head but there was no laziness about Tehran and he went on again. Eph Smith joined in on Ocean Swell but they could make no impression on me as I pushed a good horse home. He got a pace just to his liking".

Tehran's earnings of £6,202 meant that Butters won his sixth trainers' championship whilst the Aga Khan was British flat racing Champion Owner for the eighth time.

Tehran was retired from racing to become a breeding stallion. He was not a consistent producer of top-class winners but did produce some very good horses. The best of his progeny was Tulyar, who won the Derby, Eclipse Stakes, King George VI and Queen Elizabeth Stakes and St Leger enabling Tehran to win the title of Leading sire in Great Britain and Ireland in 1952.

BOOKS PUBLISHED IN 1944

Fair Stood the Wind for France is a novel written by English author H. E. Bates. The novel was first published in 1944 and was Bates's first financial success. The title comes from the first line of "Agincourt", a poem by Michael Drayton.

The story concerns John Franklin, the pilot of a Wellington bomber, who badly injures his arm when he crash-lands the aircraft in German-occupied France during the Second World War. He and his crew make their way to an isolated farmhouse and are taken in by the family of a French farmer. Plans are made to smuggle them all back to Britain via Vichy-controlled Marseille but Franklin's conditions worsen and he remains at the farm during the hot summer weeks that follow and falls in love with the farmer's daughter Françoise. Eventually they make the hazardous journey together by rowing boat, bicycle and train.

The book was adapted into a 4-part television mini-series in 1980 for the BBC, starring David Beames as Franklin and Cécile Paoli as Françoise.

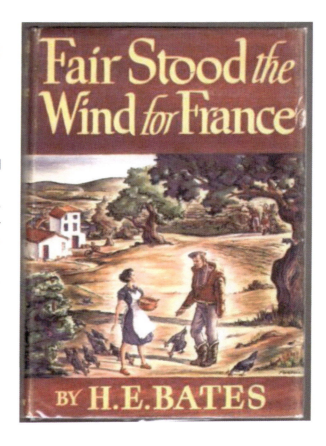

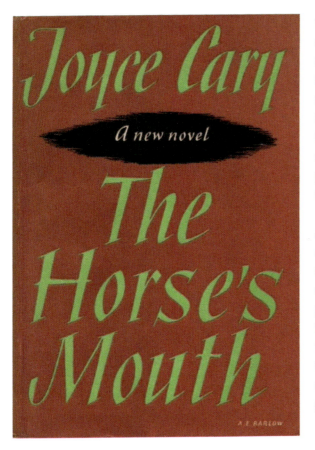

The Horse's Mouth is a 1944 novel by Anglo-Irish writer Joyce Cary, the third in his First Trilogy, whose first two books are Herself Surprised (1941) and To Be A Pilgrim (1942). The Horse's Mouth follows the adventures of Gulley Jimson, an artist who would exploit his friends and acquaintances to earn money, told from his point of view, just as the other books in the First Trilogy tell events from their central characters' different points of view. Cary's novel also uses Gulley's unique perspective to comment on the social and political events of the time.

Jimson's father, based on a real person known to Cary, was an Academy artist who is heart-broken when Impressionism drives his style from popular taste. Jimson has put aside any consideration of acceptance by either academy or public and paints in fits of creative ecstasy. Although his work is known to collectors and has become valuable, Jimson himself is forced to live from one scam or petty theft to the next. Cadging enough money to buy paints and supplies, he spends much of the novel seeking surfaces, such as walls, to serve as ground for his paintings.

Towards Zero is a work of detective fiction by Agatha Christie first published in the US by Dodd, Mead and Company in June 1944, and in the UK by the Collins Crime Club in July of the same year.

Lady Tressilian is now confined to her bed, but still invites guests to her seaside home at Gull's Point during the summer. Tennis star Nevile Strange, former ward of Lady Tressilian's deceased husband, incurs her displeasure. He proposes to bring both his new wife, Kay, and his former wife, Audrey, to visit at the same time – a change from past years. Lady Tressilian grudgingly agrees to this set of incompatible guests. Staying in hotels nearby are Kay's friend, Ted; a long-time family friend, Thomas Royde, home after a long stretch working overseas and still faithfully waiting on the side-lines for Audrey; and Mr Treves, an old solicitor and long-time friend of the Tressilians. The dinner party is uncomfortable, as Lady Tressilian had predicted. That night, Mr Treves told a story of an old case, where a child killed another child with an arrow, which was ruled an accident. The child was given a new name and a fresh start, despite a local man having seen the child practising assiduously with a bow and arrow.

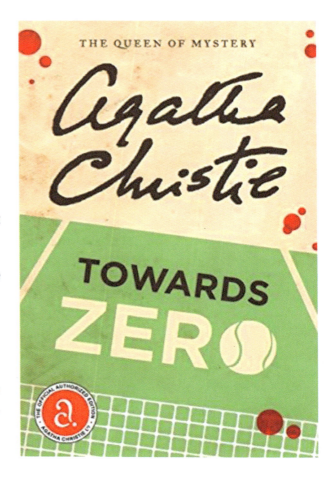

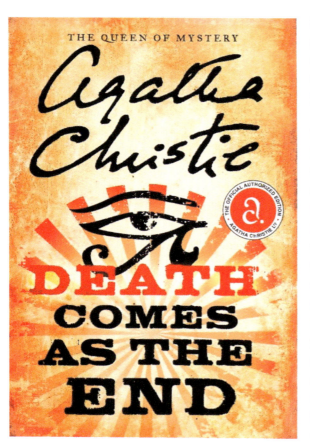

Death Comes as the End is a historical mystery novel by Agatha Christie, first published in the US by Dodd, Mead and Company in October 1944 and in the UK by the Collins Crime Club in March of the following year. The US Edition retailed at $2.00 and the UK edition at seven shillings and sixpence.

The novel is primarily written from the perspective of Renisenb, a young widow reacquainting herself with her family when her father Imhotep, a successful but pompous and short-sighted mortuary priest, brings a new "wife", Nofret, into their lives. Nofret soon disrupts and antagonises Imhotep's sons - Yahmose, Sobek and Ipy - as well as their wives. Renisenb realises the housekeeper Henet, while feigning devotion, is full of hatred. She confronts Henet near the end of the story, who in a fit of pique admits she hates Renisenb and hated Renisenb's long-deceased mother. After Imhotep is called away, Satipy and Kait, the elder sons' wives, try to bully Nofret with tricks, but the plan backfires when Nofret appeals to Imhotep and he threatens to disown his sons and their families upon his return. Suddenly everyone has a motive to kill Nofret and when she is found dead at the foot of a cliff, an accident seems unlikely, although no one will acknowledge anything else.

The Great Divorce is a novel by the British author C. S. Lewis, published in 1945, based on a theological dream vision of his in which he reflects on the Christian conceptions of Heaven and Hell.

The narrator inexplicably finds himself in a grim and joyless city, the "grey town", where it rains continuously, even indoors, which is either Hell or Purgatory depending on whether or not one stays there. He eventually finds a bus stop for those who desire an excursion to some other place (the destination later turns out to be the foothills of Heaven). He waits in line for the bus and listens to the arguments between his fellow passengers. As they await the bus's arrival, many of them quit the line in disgust before the bus pulls up. When it arrives, the driver is an angel who shields his face from the passengers. Once the few remaining passengers have boarded, the bus flies upward, off the pavement into the grey, rainy sky. The ascending bus breaks out of the rain clouds into a clear, pre-dawn sky, and as it rises its occupants' bodies change from being normal and solid into being transparent, faint, and vapor-like. When it reaches its destination the passengers on the bus – including the narrator – are gradually revealed to be ghosts.

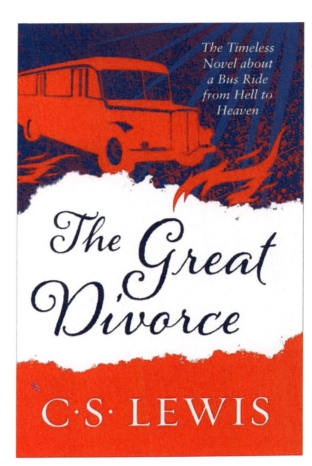

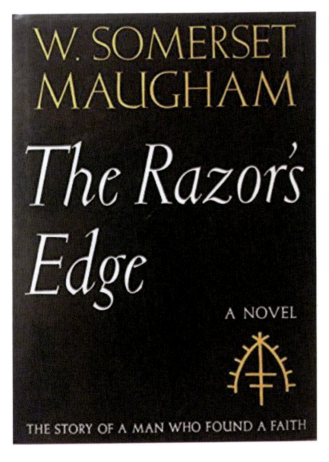

The Razor's Edge is a 1944 novel by W. Somerset Maugham. It tells the story of Larry Darrell, an American pilot traumatized by his experiences in World War I, who sets off in search of some transcendent meaning in his life. The story begins through the eyes of Larry's friends and acquaintances as they witness his personality change after the war. His rejection of conventional life and search for meaningful experience allows him to thrive while the more materialistic characters suffer reversals of fortune.

Maugham begins by characterising his story as not really a novel but a thinly veiled true account. He includes himself as a minor character, a writer who drifts in and out of the lives of the major players. Larry Darrell's lifestyle is contrasted throughout the book with that of his fiancée's uncle Elliott Templeton, an American expatriate living in Paris and an unrepentantly shallow yet generous snob. For example, while Templeton's Roman Catholicism embraces the hierarchical trappings of the church, Larry's proclivities tend towards the thirteenth-century Flemish mystic and saint John of Ruysbroeck.

MOVIE'S 1944

"Arsenic and Old Lace". The year is 1941. The location is a small house next to a cemetery in Brooklyn. In this house live two kind, thoughtful, sweet old ladies, Martha and Abby Brewster who have developed a very bad habit. It appears that they murder lonely old men who have some sort of religious affiliation and they consider doing it a charity. They then leave it to their bugle blowing nephew Teddy (who thinks he's Teddy Roosevelt) to take them to the Panama Canal (the cellar) and bury them. In this instance, the "poor fellow" suffers from yellow fever found in the window seat.

It is another of their nephews Mortimer Brewster, a dramatic critic, who returns home only to find the man in the seat by mistake. Another nephew, Jonathon, returns to the home after years of fleeing the authorities due to his "unofficial practice" of killing people and using their faces to change his. However, the results cause him to look like Boris Karloff due to the poor craftsmanship of his German accented, alcoholic sidekick Dr. Einstein.

Run Time 1hr 58Mins

Trivia

Cary Grant's (birth name), Archie Leach appears on a tombstone in the cemetery near the Brewster's house. In Grant's earlier picture, His Girl Friday (1940), his character, Walter, responded to a threat by saying 'listen, the last man that said that to me was Archie Leach, just a week before he cut his throat'. As a gag, the 'departed' Mr. Leach was apparently interred in the Brooklyn cemetery by the Brewster's home.

Cary Grant considered his acting in this film to be horribly over the top and often called it his least favourite of all his movies.

Frank Capra was forced to pay $25,000 apiece to the Broadway play's producers for their loaning Jean Adair and Josephine Hull to the film.

Goofs

As the film opens, the narration on screen tells viewers that the action begins at 3:00 PM. However, when Mortimer & Elaine go up to the window at the marriage bureau, the clerk says "Good morning, children."

Just before Jonathan and Dr. Einstein show up, Aunt Abby arranges the two candelabras so that they are both facing forward. After Jonathan and Dr. Einstein enter, one of the candelabras is facing sideways.

The movie opens with the Brooklyn Dodgers winning a baseball game on Halloween, weeks after the end of baseball season. This is a gag to suggest that the only time the Brooklyn Dodgers could win is on Halloween, similar to saying when pigs fly.

When Jonathan runs his thumb along the edge of the surgical knife, it does not actually touch the blade.

"Gaslight" In London, at 9 Thorton Square, prima donna Alice Alquist is strangled, and her famous jewels disappear. Her young niece Paula Alquist (Terry Moore) is sent to Italy to study music, and the house stays empty. Ten years later, Paula (Ingrid Bergman) decides to get married with an older pianist named Gregory Anton (Charles Boyer), who convinces her to move back to the old address in London. When they arrive, Paula finds a letter from a mysterious and unknown Sergis Bauer, which makes Gregory upset. He psychologically begins to torture Paula, and she has a nervous breakdown, and also has insecurity and memory problems. When Scotland Yard Police Constable Brian Cameron (Joseph Cotten) sees Gregory and Alice in a place popular with tourists, he immediately he sees Paula, who reminds him of her aunt, but he does not know Gregory, and decides to investigate and find evidence to connect Gregory with the unsolved murder, while Paula is being driven insane and menaced by her husband. The opening and closing credits are displayed over a background of a burning gaslight. If you look at the shadow on the wallpaper, you see a man strangling a woman.

Run time is 1h 54mins

Trivia

Director George Cukor suggested that Ingrid Bergman study the patients at a mental hospital to learn about nervous breakdowns. She did, focusing on one woman in particular, whose habits and physical quirks became part of the character.

This movie won an Academy Award for set decoration. The gas oilers were real and the one in Charles Boyer's bedroom came from the 1872 Menlo Park, California mansion of Senator Milton Latham, which was torn down in 1942.

Ingrid Bergman spent some time in a mental institution to research her role, studying a woman who had suffered a nervous breakdown.

Goofs

Gregory is shown leaving the house from the inside, opening the door most of the way. The following shot, showing the next moment outside, repeats most of the door-opening.

The guide in the Tower of London is incorrectly shown as wearing the uniform of the Chelsea pensioners instead of the Yeoman guard.

At the beginning, a man is lighting outdoor gaslights on tall poles, using a long pole with a flame on the end. He is shown lighting one light, then a close-up of the next one shows the end of the pole entering the gaslight glass enclosure, but it has no flame for starting the light. That shot ends before the starter pole lights the light.

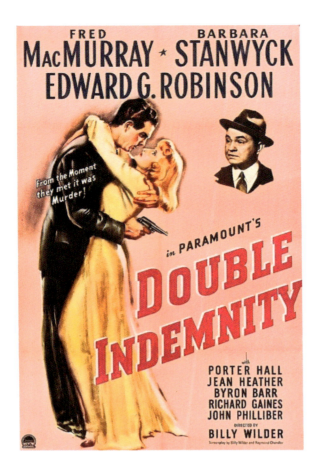

"Double Indemnity". Alone in his company's Los Angeles offices late one evening and under some distress, insurance salesman Walter Neff dictates an inter-office memo to his colleague, claims manager Barton Keyes, about killing one of his clients, a Mr. Dietrichson. Barton suspected that Dietrichson was murdered by his wife, Phyllis Dietrichson, who was claiming the double indemnity on her husband's accident insurance policy. Walter met Phyllis innocently enough - he was dropping off auto insurance renewal papers for her husband - but quickly fell under her seductive charms. They were obvious to each other in their mutual attraction. After deducing that she was planning on killing her husband since she stated he was abusive and claiming the insurance moneys on a policy her husband would have no idea existed, Walter decided to go into cahoots with her so that he could help her craft and execute the "perfect" insurance policy, and plan and execute the "perfect" murder beyond Keyes' scrutiny, leading to them living in bliss together and with money.

Run Time 1h 47mins

Trivia

The house used as Barbara Stanwyck's character's home still stands today at 6301 Quebec Drive.

Edward G. Robinson's initial reluctance to sign on largely stemmed from the fact he wasn't keen on being demoted to third lead. Eventually, he realized that he was at a transitional phase of his career, plus the fact that he was getting paid the same as Barbara Stanwyck and Fred MacMurray for doing less work.

The blonde wig that Barbara Stanwyck is wearing throughout the movie was the idea of Billy Wilder. A month into shooting Wilder suddenly realized how bad it looked, but by then it was too late to re-shoot the earlier scenes. To rationalize this mistake, in later interviews Wilder claimed that the bad-looking wig was intentional.

Fred MacMurray's reputation at the time was for playing nice guys, so he didn't feel he was up to the challenge. Dogged persistence on Billy Wilder's part eventually wore him down.

Goofs

The movie is set in 1938, but at Stanwyck's house the radio is playing "Tangerine" which wasn't written until 1942.

After Neff meets with the President of his company, he returns to his apartment and places a folder on the chair to the right of the door. When Keyes comes to the door, after Neff's brief phone conversation, the folder is nowhere to be seen.

Although set in 1938, Walter Neff refers to the "The Philadelphia Story", which did not debut on Broadway until 1939, and on film until 1940.

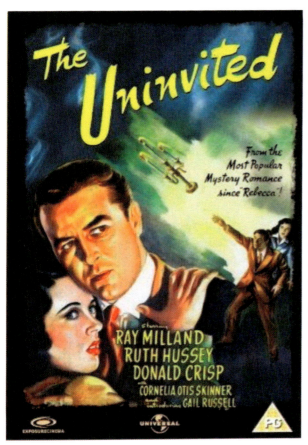

"The Uninvited". When brother and sister Roderick and Pamela Fitzgerald stumble across a vacant old house on the west of England, they know they have to buy it. They're forewarned by the owner, Commander Beech, that there have been strange occurrences there but they go ahead anyway. The house had once belonged to Beech's daughter, Mary Meredith, who committed suicide by jumping off the nearby cliff and his granddaughter Stella Meredith, now a young woman, lived there until she was 3 years old. Roderick and Pamela pay no mind to the rumours and tall tales but soon find that there are spirits in the house. They become convinced that the spirit is that of Beech's daughter but it is clear that the target of her venom is her own daughter Stella. Beech is convinced that his granddaughter is in danger in that house and seeks the assistance of the family's one-time nurse, Miss Holloway. She too however, seems to have her own secrets. With the assistance of the local doctor, Dr. Scott, they unearth the truth of what happened all those years ago.

Run time 1h 39mins

Trivia

Moyna MacGill (who is Angela Lansbury's mother) has an uncredited role as the customer who enters the cigar shop while Roderick is speaking with the proprietor.

When Stella enters a trance and speaks in Spanish during the seance, she says, "Listen, listen! It's not her! It's not her! Do not believe anything! Do not listen to her, because she's lying! You thief! Thief of my love!"

Paramount added special effects to the film, having decided at the last moment to emphasize its "supernatural premise." The effects were removed by censors when the film was distributed in England.

In 2009 Martin Scorsese placed this film on his list of the 11 scariest horror films of all time.

Goofs

The film is set in 1937, but the "going-to-church" sequence features a car with headlights blacked out in the style required due to WWII in the early 1940s.

Rick was eating an apple before bed. He placed it on the bedside table. Upon arising hearing the cries, you see the table without the apple core. After he returns to bed you clearly see the apple core on the table.

When Roderick & Stella are sailing in a small boat, they did the old chestnut of hitting him on the back of the head with the boom. However, Stella pushed the tiller. That would have sent the boom to starboard, away from Roderick's head. Background didn't shift either.

Ray Milland's lips do not move when he says, "I should think so. It had nursery wallpaper."

"The Canterville Ghost". In 1634, in England, Sir Simon de Canterville agrees to take his wounded brother Anthony's place in a duel with the diminutive Sir Valentine Williams. The portly Simon demands that the duel be fought with lances, but to his horror, Sir Valentine also claims injury and sends his enormous cousin to the duel in his stead. After the first pass, a terrified Simon flees on his horse and hides in an alcove in the Canterville castle. Valentine pursues him there, but Simon's proud father, Lord Canterville, insists that his son would not tarnish the family name by hiding. As proof of Simon's courage, Lord Canterville agrees to have the alcove bricked up and, despite Simon's pleas, condemns him to die in the tomb and walk the castle's halls until a Canterville descendent commits a brave act while wearing Simon's signet ring. In 1943, the now-deserted Canterville castle, with its infamous ghost, Simon, is besieged by a platoon of American soldiers, who are to be billeted there. The castle's current owner, the precocious six-year-old Lady Jessica de Canterville, who lives nearby with her aunt, Mrs. Polverdine, greets the soldiers and tells them about the castle's haunting.

Run time 1h 35mins

Trivia

This is the 2nd film that Robert Young was in with Margaret O'Brien. The 1st was "Journey for Margaret" (1942). Both of them took place in England around WWII and in both he played an American and she was British.

"Lux Radio Theatre" broadcast a 60-minute radio adaptation of the movie on June 18, 1945 with Charles Laughton and Margaret O'Brien reprising their film roles.

Some cast members in studio records/casting call lists did not appear or were not identifiable in the movie. These were (with their character names): David Thursby (Carpenter), Larry Wheat (Doctor) and Billy Bletcher (Window Washer). A contemporary news item listed Ethel Griffies as a cast member, but she was not seen in the movie either.

Goofs

When the soldier hiding inside the suit of armour (to take the ghost's photo) falls over, he falls on his face. In the next shot he is on his back, with the other soldiers surrounding him.

While many German parachute mines with time delay dropped on England during World War II; but they weren't called blockbusters. The blockbuster was a type of bomb devised by the British. At first a blockbuster was a four-thousand-pound bomb; but later became an 8000 and then a 12000-pound bomb. They achieved these sizes by simply bolting two or three of the 4000 pounders together. They were called Blockbusters because it was calculated that they could destroy a city block.

All through the movie, the ghost walks through walls, doors, etc. One of the soldiers ties a string to his toe and runs the other end to the stairway to alert him when the ghost is moving about the castle.

"Meet Me in St Louis".
Judy Garland stars in a timeless tale of family, captured with warmth and emotion by director Vincente Minnelli. The enduring popularity of Meet Me in St. Louis comes from a terrific blend of music, romance and humour. Starring Judy Garland, together with Margaret O'Brien (awarded a special Oscar as 1944's outstanding child actress) and Mary Astor, and featuring the musical classics "Meet Me in St. Louis, Louis," "The Trolley Song" and "Have Yourself a Merry Little Christmas." St. Louis 1903.

The well-off Smith family has four beautiful daughters, including Esther and little Tootie. Seventeen-year old Esther has fallen in love with John, the boy next door who has just moved in. He, however, barely notices her at first. The family is shocked when Mr. Smith reveals that he has been transferred to a nice position in New York, which means that the family has to leave St. Louis just before the start of the St. Louis 1904 World's Fair.

Run time 1h 53mins

Trivia

This film was a box-office smash, grossing more money than any prior MGM release in 20 years with the exception of David O. Selznick's Gone with the Wind (1939).

The book on which the film is based originally ran as a weekly feature in the New Yorker Magazine in 1942. For the film, many of the actions attributed to Tootie were actually done in real life by Sally Benson's sister Agnes. Also, in reality, Benson's father moved the family to NYC, and they never did come back for the World's Fair. Twenty years later, Benson would have sole screenwriting credit on Elvis Presley's biggest box office hit, 1964's Viva Las Vegas.

Judy Garland missed 13 days of work, causing the production to take 70 days to complete instead of the original budgeted 58 days.

Goofs

On Halloween night, Agnes and Tootie walk up to the children having the bonfire. When they ask who it is, Agnes incorrectly says, "It's me! Angus!"

When Esther and Tootie perform "Under the Bamboo Tree", Tootie's bedroom slippers are pink at the beginning of the number but change to blue in the "cake walk" finale.

In the supper scene when they are trying to rush the meal so that Rose can take her long-distance call in private, Katie the maid serves Mr. Smith his soup. The bowl looks completely empty through the whole scene until Katie comes to pick up the bowl. At that point, it is full of brightly-coloured soup.

The piece of cake that Mr. Smith eats for Halloween dessert starts out flat and later grows into a wedge.

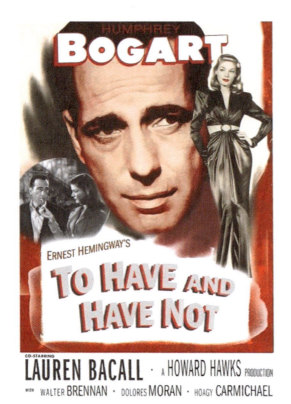

"To Have and Have Not". The tense situation in Nazi occupied France also hits the French colony Martinique in the Caribbean. In its capital Fort de France an American sea captain, Harry Morgan, has some trouble with the local authorities, who is all the time spying on possible collaborators of the resistance movement. But Harry Morgan is a recluse, who doesn't want to be involved in anything. He keeps all persons at a distance, except the alcoholic sailor Eddie, who he cares for. A young woman, Marie Browning, age 22, moves into Hotel Marquis in the room opposite his. She immediately captures his interest, and she is also affected by him. Morgan thinks this isn't a proper milieu for a young woman, and wants to help her get back home. To be able to pay her flight ticket, he contacts the resistance movement, saying he accepts transporting two persons from Anguilla to Martinique with his fishing boat in the night, if he is well paid. During the operation they are spotted by a patrol boat, but Morgan extinguishes their lantern by a gunshot, and slips away with his boat.

Run time 1h 40mins

Trivia

At the funeral for her husband, Humphrey Bogart, Lauren Bacall put a whistle in his coffin. It was a reference to the famous line in the film where she says to him: "You know how to whistle, don't you? You just put your lips together and blow."

Dolores Moran was originally scripted to be the lead actress and Humphrey Bogart's romantic interest, but her role was shrunk to make room for Lauren Bacall.

According to a biography of William Faulkner, he was the sole author of the "second revised final" script, but Hawks changed so much of the story to suit his own style that little of Faulkner's work remained.

The first of four films made by real-life couple and later husband and wife Humphrey Bogart and Lauren Bacall.

Goofs

When Frenchy takes Capt. Morgan to the cellar to remove a bullet, Frenchy unlocks the cellar door and promptly relocks it after they enter the cellar. A few minutes later, Slim comes down the stairs in the cellar with the first aid kit and the hot water. Frenchy has been in the room with the wounded man all this time and couldn't have unlocked the cellar door.

When Harry Morgan is sitting in the bar, the bottle on his table moves around and disappears between shots.

When Slim walks over to the piano to say goodbye to Cricket there is a crowd gathered around the piano watching them but as the scene goes through various edits, the make-up of the crowd and the positioning of some of the people in the crowd keep changing.

The musical group sings in Spanish even though they're in a French province.

"House of Frankenstein". Dr. Niemann regales his hunchbacked cellmate, Daniel, with tales of how he had nearly put the brain of a human into a dog. This gives Daniel hope. If brain switches are possible, that would mean his own brain could be removed to a better home than the misshapen body he's now trapped in. A thunderstorm destroys their prison, and they escape to find refuge in the company of a traveling carnival. The carnival owner has possession of the skeleton of Count Dracula, who can be revived by removing the wooden stake from the area of his heart. Niemann has the hunchback kill the owner, and then resurrects Dracula to kill those who had sent him to prison. But Dracula has other plans. Later, Niemann and the hunchback encounter a gypsy caravan where Daniel falls in love with a beautiful gypsy girl. She travels with them to Frankenstein's ruined castle, where they find Frankenstein's monster and the Wolf Man frozen in ice. Niemann thaws them out, finding the Monster fairly inert and the Wolf Man changed back to the tormented Larry Talbot. To Daniel's misery, the gypsy girl falls in love with Talbot, unaware of his lupine alter ego.

Run time 1h 11mins

Trivia

Bela Lugosi was slated for the role of Dracula, but the film was dependent upon the presence of Boris Karloff being released from the stage tour of Arsenic and Old Lace (1944). Shooting was delayed, and John Carradine was cast instead of Lugosi, who had a prior engagement: ironically, playing Karloff's "Jonathan Brewster" role in another touring company of "Arsenic and Old Lace."

In his scenes with John Carradine, Peter Coe described in an interview how Carradine found ways to upstage him and steal the scene. After Coe confronted and threatened him if it happened again, he said Carradine became more co-operative and professional.

Glenn Strange was the fourth actor to play the Monster in Universal's Frankenstein series. The actor who played the original Monster, Boris Karloff, was also present in the film, playing the role of Dr. Niemann. Being on the set, Karloff was able to personally coach Strange in the way the Monster should be played.

Goofs

Right after Dracula's carriage crashes he can be seen in the background running towards his coffin but in the next shot he is sitting on the ground.

As the Wolfman thaws, his right hand is on his stomach and his left hand is on his chest. A single dissolve, and he is back to being Lawrence Talbot, but his hands have switched position - right hand on chest, left hand on stomach.

When Larry Talbot emerges from the ice, his clothes are perfectly dry and pressed.

When Larry Talbot transforms into the Wolf Man for the final time, his hands aren't made up. This can be spotted before he crashes through the glass door.

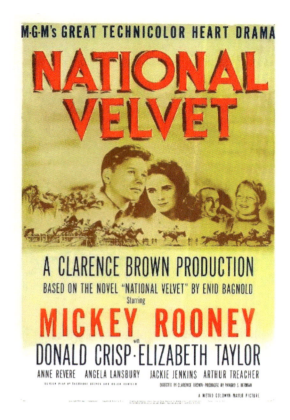

"National Velvet". In the English coastal village of Sewels in Sussex, 12-year-old Velvet Brown and her older sisters, Edwina and Malvolia, happily finish their last day of school before summer vacation. While walking home, Velvet meets young drifter Mi Taylor and strikes up a conversation with him. As the horse-crazy girl is talking to Mi, she sees a beautiful, rambunctious gelding being chased by its owner, farmer Ede, and is awestruck. When Ede then questions Mi about his business in Sewels in Sussex, Velvet, who is impressed by Mi's knowledge of horses, insists that he has been invited to dine with her family. That evening at dinner, Mrs. Brown asks Mi, whom she has never before met, about an address book with her name written in it, and he reveals that it belonged to his now-deceased father. Although Mrs. Brown is deliberately secretive about her relationship with Mi's father, she does invite Mi to spend the night in the stable. Velvet then tries in vain to convince her father Herbert, a butcher who prides himself on his thrift and self-control, to hire Mi as a delivery boy. When he and his wife discuss the matter later, however, the wise, persuasive Mrs. Brown easily changes his mind.

Run time 2h 3mins

Trivia

Dame Elizabeth Taylor fell from the horse and broke her back during the filming of the racing scene. Although she recovered quickly, she suffered greatly later in life.

Mickey Rooney had to film all of his scenes in one month before he had to report for basic training to serve in World War II.

After production was completed, arrangements were made to allow Dame Elizabeth Taylor to keep the horse. She kept the horse from age 13 until it died when she was 24.

King Charles, playing The Pie, was first-cousin of champion thoroughbred Seabiscuit, subject of two biopics. Both had Man o' War as grand-sire.

Goofs

The horses are shown turning right at one point during the race. All turns on the Grand National course are made to the left.

In the book, the Pie, was short for piebald, an English term for black-and-white horses. The Pie was discriminated against in the book because of the piebald colour.

The story takes place in the late-1920s, and the Browns pay the entry fee with "100 gold sovereigns" which ceased to be used as money in England in 1918. However, this is consistent with a detail from the novel, in which Mrs Brown insists the entry fee be paid with the sovereigns she won swimming the English Channel, which occurred prior to 1918.

The Grand National is over fences. The jumps in the movie's version of the race are hurdles.

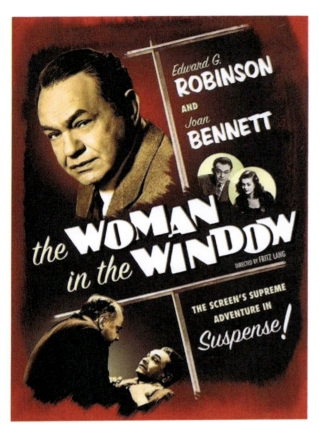

"The Woman in the Window" When the family of Gotham College Professor Richard Wanley travels, he meets with his close friends Dr. Michael Barkstane and District Attorney Frank Lalor in a club for talking. Wanley is fascinated with the portrait of a young woman in the next-door window, and they discuss about affairs and middle-age crisis while drinking. When Wanley leaves the club, he walks to the window to admire the picture once more and he meets Alice Reed, who was the model of the painting. She invites him for a drink and they end the night in her apartment for seeing sketches of Alice made by the same artist. While drinking champagne, her temper able lover arrives and misunderstands the presence of Richard, hitting and suffocating him. In self-defence, Richard stabs the man with a pair of scissors on the back and kills him. They decide to get rid of the body, dumping the body in the woods and destroying the evidences, but when they are blackmailed by the scum Heidt, Professor Wanley tells Alice that there are only three ways to deal with a blackmailer, all of them with a high price.

Run time 1h 47mins

Trivia

The painting of Alice Reed was done by Paul Clemens. He painted portraits of many Hollywood stars, often with their children. He was married to Eleanor Parker from 1954 to 1965.

Former "Our Gang" members George 'Spanky' McFarland and Robert Blake (Mickey Gubitosi) both have cameo appearances. They did not have any scenes together. Spanky, (who is 16) plays a bespectacled Boy Scout on a newsreel who discovers Manzard's corpse, while Blake appears early on in the picture as Professor Wanley's little boy, Dickie, departing the train station with his mother and sister, Elsie.

Although plausible in Wanley perhaps knowing all in his dream, he never personally meets Heidt in his dream, but shows recognition to Tim, the coat check guy, as being the doppelganger of Heidt.

Goofs

When Wanley is hurrying back into the apartment through the rain, his hat and coat are clearly soaked. In the next shot, when he is inside, his clothes are considerably less rain-soaked than before.

When Claude Mazard hits Alice in the face, his hand clearly does not actually hit her, yet she reacts to it.

In the end of the movie, Professor Wanley stares at Heidt/Tim the Doorman with the same recognition as he does with Claude Mazard/Charlie the Hatcheck man, despite his character having no interaction with Heidt in the dream sequence, which would seem to be a goof. However, if in his dream he saw everything as if watching a film or in the third person, this would make sense.

Claude Mazard is stabbed in the back with scissors multiple times, yet there is clearly no wound when he falls to the floor.

"Going my Way" Father Fitzgibbon has been the parish priest at St. Dominic's in New York City for forty-five years. The parish faces financial and social problems which the diocese believes cannot be solved by Father Fitzgibbon's traditional and conservative approach to running the parish. The bishop appoints progressive Father O'Malley, originally from St. Louis, to, on the surface, assist Father Fitzgibbon at St. Dominic's. In reality, Father O'Malley has been appointed to lead the parish out of these problems, something that Father Fitzgibbon is unaware, and something that Father O'Malley does not want to divulge in letting Father Fitzgibbon continue his work in dignity. Father O'Malley's task is made all the more difficult as Father Fitzgibbon does not approve of Father O'Malley's ways, both as priest and as a person. In general, Father Fitzgibbon takes a rather strict approach typical to the traditional ways of the church, whereas Father O'Malley takes a more compassionate humanistic approach, he who wants to bring people back to the church through more contemporary means rather than the old "fire and brimstone" preaching.

Run time 2h 6mins

Trivia

Bing Crosby sang "Swinging on a Star" by Jimmy Van Heusen, which went on to win an Academy Award for Best Song. Crosby sang four different Oscar-winning songs in his films.

Banned in several Latin American countries because Bing Crosby wore a white shirt as a priest.

Filmed in St. Monica Catholic Church near the beach in Santa Monica, California. Leo McCarey based the Barry Fitzgerald character in part on the church's real (irascible) pastor, Msgnr. Nicholas Conneally.

The first film to win Best Picture at both the Academy Awards and the Golden Globe Awards.

Goofs

When Father O'Malley is talking to Jenny while she is getting ready to perform, the conductor can be seen taking out his cigarette case and opening it twice, in two adjacent shots.

In the scene in Carol's apartment, when father O'Malley enters you can see a crew member's hand close the door behind him.

After seeing the bishop, Father Fitzgibbon calls Father O'Malley into his office where they have a long talk. There's a clock in the background, often seen over O'Malley's shoulder. From the first and last time you see it about three minutes goes by, but the clock always says 5:35.

Directly after the first rendition of "Going My Way", the shadow of the boom mic can be seen moving on the church wall behind father Fitzgibbon and Miss Linden.

Shadow of mic visible behind Ted when Father O'Malley goes to Carol's apartment.

MUSIC 1944

Artist	Single	Reached number one	Weeks at number one
		1944	
The Mills Brothers	"Paper Doll"	1st January 1944	12
The Andrews Sisters	"Shoo-Shoo Baby"	15th January 1944	8
The Merry Macs	"Mairzy Doats"	18th March 1944	5
Guy Lombardo and His Royal Canadians	"It's Love-Love-Love"	22nd April 1944	2
Bing Crosby with John Scott Trotter	"I Love You"	3rd June 1944	5
Harry James and His Orchestra	"I'll Get By"	10th June 1944	4
Bing Crosby with John Scott Trotter	"I'll Be Seeing You"	6th May 1944	5
Bing Crosby with John Scott Trotter	"Swinging on a Star"	5th August 1944	9
The Mills Brothers	"You Always Hurt the One You Love"	7th October 1944	1
Dinah Shore	"I'll Walk Alone"	14th October 1944	1
The Mills Brothers	"You Always Hurt the One You Love"	21th October 1944	2
Dinah Shore	"I'll Walk Alone"	4th November 1944	3
The Mills Brothers	"You Always Hurt the One You Love"	25th November 1944	2
The Ink Spots and Ella Fitzgerald	"I'm Making Believe"	9th December 1944	2
Bing Crosby and the Andrews Sisters	"Don't Fence Me In"	23rd December 1944	2

In 1944, as in previous years, Bing Crosby ruled the charts. Seven songs make this list, and we could lobby for one or two others. Ask most people who was the biggest singing star of the 1940s, and the universal answer is Frank Sinatra. Ol' Blue Eyes had his hits, to be sure, and his mere presence created near-riot situations around the country. But it was Der Bingle who ruled the charts. Sinatra was the "Elvis" of his day, except he didn't garner nearly as many number one records as Presley would a dozen years later.

Two unlikely groups also defined the decade. First one that comes to mind is The Andrews Sisters. Their vocal style and all-American spirit worked perfectly during the war years. They were just as comfortable fronting Glenn Miller as Desi Arnaz, working a song with Abbott & Costello or Guy Lombardo. They worked with bandleader Bob Crosby and then went on to record 47 songs with his brother, the aforementioned Bing. Of those 47 songs, 23 made it to the charts. A lot of sister vocal teams have followed, but none have come close to Maxene, Patty, and LaVerne.

The Mills Brothers

"Paper Doll"

"Paper Doll" was a hit song for The Mills Brothers. In the United States it held the number-one position on the Billboard singles chart for twelve weeks from 6th November 1943 to 22nd January 1944. The success of the song represented something of a revival for the group after a few years of declining sales. It is one of the fewer than 40 all-time singles to have sold 10 million (or more) physical copies worldwide. On 18th February 1942, The Mills Brothers recorded "I'll Be Around" by Alec Wilder as their new single, with "Paper Doll" as the B-side. It is rumoured that it took less than fifteen minutes to record the latter. Harry Mills recalled that he and his brother Herbert did not initially like the song, although their brother Donald did. However, Harry said, "as we went along rehearsing it, we got to feeling it".

The Andrews Sisters

"Shoo-Shoo Baby"

"Shoo Shoo Baby" is a popular song written by Phil Moore. The song was made famous by The Andrews Sisters as they sang it in the 1943 film Three Cheers for the Boys. "Shoo, Shoo Baby" was a big hit for the trio in 1944, reaching No. 6 in the chart. Their version features a jazzy vocal pop arrangement typical of the time, with a key hook provided by the horns. It was and has appeared on many albums' of 1940s music.

Ella Mae Morse also recorded this song in 1943, with Dick Walters and His Orchestra. A version of the song by an uncredited male singer is played over a radio at the Heavenly trial of the airman in the 1946 film A Matter of Life and Death as a symbol of modern America. This song was also the inspiration for the naming of the Shoo Shoo Baby, a B-17 Flying Fortress which served during World War II.

The Merry Macs

"Mairzy Doats"

"Mairzy Doats" is a novelty song written and composed in 1943 by Milton Drake, Al Hoffman, and Jerry Livingston. It contains lyrics that make no sense as written, but are near homophones of meaningful phrases. The song's title, for example, is a homophone of "Mares eat oats".

The song was first played on radio station WOR, New York, by Al Trace and his Silly Symphonists. It made the pop charts several times, with a version by the Merry Macs reaching No. 1 in March 1944. The song was also a number-one sheet music seller, with sales of over 450,000 within the first three weeks of release. The Merry Macs recording was Decca Records' best-selling release in 1944. Twenty-three other performers followed up with their own recordings in a span of only two weeks that year.

Guy Lombardo and his Royal Canadians

"It's Love-Love-Love"

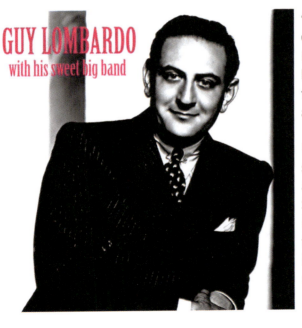

"It's Love-Love-Love" The best-known recording was by Guy Lombardo and his Royal Canadians (vocal by Skip Nelson). It was recorded on 7th January 1944, and released by Decca Records as catalog number 18589. It first reached the Billboard magazine Best Seller chart on 6th April 6 1944 and lasted 10 weeks on the chart, peaking at #1.

Unfortunately, the ubiquitous Guy Lombardo Billboard #1 single recording omits the charming third verse, which is arguably the most amusing in this short, humorous ditty. Sirius XM Forties Junction occasionally plays a recording (such as the RCA Victor Four King Sisters one) that has all three verses performed just as written, but it is rare to hear it, hard to find on YouTube, nor does iTunes offer a recording other than the Guy Lombardo 1944 version.

Bing Crosby with John Scott Trotter

"I Love You"

"I Love You" is a song written by Cole Porter in 1944 for his stage musical Mexican Hayride. The New York Times reviewed the show, saying, among other things: "Of Mr. Porter's score, the best number bears the title almost startling in its forthrightness, "I Love You," and is the property of Mr. Evans". However, the rather generic lyrics of the song were due to a challenge given by Porter. His friend Monty Woolley contended that Porter's talent lay in the off-beat and the esoteric, maintaining that he could never take a cliché title like "I Love You" and write lyrics that included the banal sentiment: "It's spring again, and birds on the wing again" and be successful. Porter accepted the challenge with the result that the song eventually topped the hit parade. Porter remarked that the "superior melody overcame the ordinary lyric".

Harry James and his Orchestra

"I'll Get By (As Long as I Have You)"

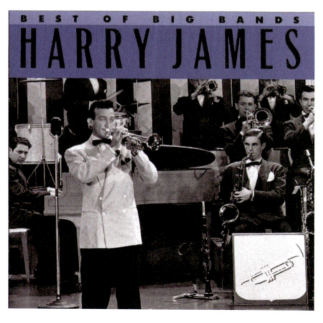

"I'll Get By (As Long as I Have You)" In 1944 the song achieved its biggest success with a version by Harry James and His Orchestra featuring vocalist Dick Haymes – an April 1941 recording re-released owing to a stipulation by the 1942–44 musicians' strike that prevented recording of new material. The single debuted in April 1944 on Billboard's National Best-Selling Retail Records chart and reached number one in the chart dated 10th June 1944 – the seventh of Harry James's nine US number ones. It stayed at number one for four non-consecutive weeks. The single topped Billboard's Most Played Juke Box Records chart for six weeks. A recording by The Ink Spots featuring tenor Bill Kenny also reached Billboard's Top Ten in 1944. A version by the King Sisters peaked at no. 12. The song featured in the Variety chart 10 Best Sellers on Coin-Machines in the week dated 12th June 1944.

Bing Crosby

"I'll Be Seeing You"

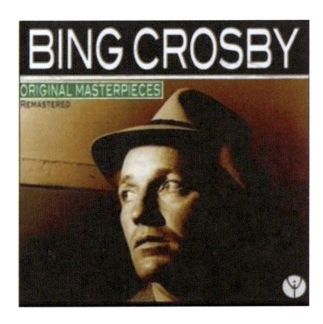

"I'll Be Seeing You" is a popular song about missing a loved one, with music by Sammy Fain and lyrics by Irving Kahal. Published in 1938, it was inserted into the Broadway musical Right This Way, which closed after fifteen performances. The title of the 1944 film I'll Be Seeing You was taken from this song at the suggestion of the film's producer, Dore Schary. The song is included in the film's soundtrack. The recording by Bing Crosby became a hit in 1944, reaching number one for the week of 1st July. Frank Sinatra's version with Tommy Dorsey and His Orchestra from 1940 charted in 1944 and peaked at No. 4. A new recording of the song by Frank Sinatra was included in 1961's I Remember Tommy. This new version went to No. 12 on the Easy Listening chart and No. 58 on the Hot 100.

Bing Crosby

"Swinging on a Star"

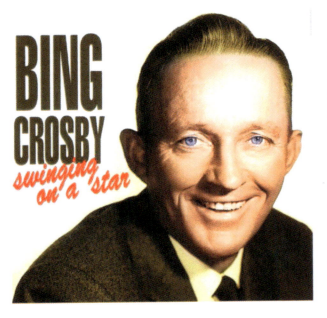

"Swinging on a Star" is an American pop standard with music composed by Jimmy Van Heusen and lyrics by Johnny Burke. It was introduced by Bing Crosby in the 1944 film Going My Way, winning an Academy Award for Best Original Song that year and has been recorded by numerous artists since then. In 2004, it finished at No. 37 in AFI's 100 Years...100 Songs survey of top tunes in American cinema. The first recording of "Swinging on a Star", with Bing Crosby with John Scott Trotter and His Orchestra, took place in Los Angeles on February 7, 1944, and was released as Decca Records on Disc No. 18597 paired with "Going My Way". The song topped the USA charts in 1944 and Australian charts in 1945. The Williams Brothers Quartet, including a young Andy Williams, sang backup vocals behind Crosby.

The Mills Brothers

"You Always Hurt the One You Love"

"You Always Hurt the One You Love" is a pop standard, with words by Allan Roberts and music by Doris Fisher. First recorded by The Mills Brothers, whose recording reached the top of the Billboard charts in 1944, it was also a hit for Sammy Kaye (vocal by Billy Williams) in 1945. It has been performed by many other artists over the years, including Moon Mullican with Cliff Bruner, Connie Francis, Fats Domino, The Impressions, Molly Nilsson, George Maharis, Frankie Laine, Richard Chamberlain, Peggy Lee, Maureen Evans, Michael Bublé, Kay Starr, Hank Thompson, Ringo Starr (in his 1970 album Sentimental Journey), and Clarence "Frogman" Henry, whose version became a top 20 hit on the Billboard Hot 100 in 1961. It was also popular in a parody version by Spike Jones. The song was performed by Ryan Gosling and featured prominently in the 2010 film Blue Valentine.

Dinah Shore

"I'll Walk Alone"

"I'll Walk Alone" is a 1944 popular song with music by Jule Styne and lyrics by Sammy Cahn. The song was written for the 1944 musical film Follow the Boys, in which it was sung by Dinah Shore, and was nominated for the Academy Award for Best Original Song but lost to "Swinging on a Star". Shore recorded the song in March as a single, which became her first #1 hit on the Billboard charts. "I'll Walk Alone" was released in May 1944 and first appeared in 'The Billboard' on June 3, 1944. Competing versions were released by Martha Tilton, Mary Martin, Louis Prima, and others. It finally reached the top ten of the Best Selling and "Most Played Juke Box Records" charts in August 1944. Despite charting with Bing Crosby's "Swinging on A Star", "I'll Walk Alone" remained in the top ten of the Best-Selling Records chart for twenty consecutive weeks, with four of those as the number one song in the nation.

The Ink Spots and Ella Fitzgerald

"I'm Making Believe"

"I'm Making Believe" is a 1944 song composed by James V. Monaco with lyrics by Mack Gordon. The song first appeared in the film Sweet and Low-Down; the performance by Benny Goodman and His Orchestra was nominated for the Academy Award for Best Original Song. The version recorded by the Ink Spots and Ella Fitzgerald topped The Billboard's National Best-Selling Retail Records chart for two weeks in 1944. Their version had sold over one million copies by the time of Fitzgerald's death in 1996. On 30th August 1944, Ella Fitzgerald and the vocal group the Ink Spots recorded the vocals for "I'm Making Believe" and "Into Each Life Some Rain Must Fall" in New York City for producer Milt Gabler. "I'm Making Believe" was recorded with two opposing choruses by Fitzgerald and Ink Spots member Bill Kenny.

Bing Crosby and the Andrew Sisters

"Don't Fence Me In"

"Don't Fence Me In" is a popular American song written in 1934, with music by Cole Porter and lyrics by Robert Fletcher and Cole Porter. Members of the Western Writers of America chose it as one of the Top 100 Western songs of all time. Originally written in 1934 for Adios, Argentina, an unproduced 20th Century Fox film musical, "Don't Fence Me In" was based on text by Robert (Bob) Fletcher, a poet and engineer with the Department of Highways in Helena, Montana. Bing Crosby and The Andrews Sisters with Vic Schoen and his Orchestra recorded it in 1944, without having seen or heard the song. Crosby entered the studio on 25th July 1944. Within 30 minutes, he and the Andrews Sisters had completed the recording, which sold more than a million copies and topped the Billboard charts for eight weeks in 1944–45. This version also went to number nine on the Harlem Hit Parade chart.

WORLD EVENTS 1944

January

1st | The Syrian Republic was recognized as independent.

2nd | The Red Army captured Radovel northwest of Korosten and came within 18 miles of the pre-war Polish border.

3rd | The American destroyer USS Turner sank off the Ambrose Light in New York after suffering a series of onboard explosions. 138 of 256 crew perished.

4th | The Soviet 1st Ukrainian Front pushed Erich von Manstein's Army Group South back beyond the pre-war Polish border at Sarny.

5th | With Red Army forces about to cross the Polish border, the Polish government-in-exile issued a declaration describing itself as "the only and legal steward and spokesman of the Polish Nation" and calling for the Soviet Union to respect the rights and interests of Poland. The statement also proposed the re-establishment of a liberated republic in Poland as quickly as possible as well as the negotiation of an agreement between the Polish government-in-exile and the Soviet Union that would permit the co-ordination of Polish resistance actions with the Red Army.

8th | The Verona trial began in the Italian Social Republic. Six leading members of the Grand Council of Fascism were put on trial for voting in favour of Benito Mussolini's removal from power during the events of 25 Luglio.

10th | The Verona Trial ended with five death sentences. Tullio Cianetti was the only defendant spared from execution, in light of his having written a letter of apology to Mussolini. He was given a 30-year prison term instead.

11th | The P-51 Mustang joined the P-38 Lightning and P-47 Thunderbolt in U.S. long-range escort missions over Germany.

P-51 Mustang　　　　**P-38 Lightening**　　　　**P-47 Thunderbolt**

13th | The director of the United States Typhus Commission warned that Naples faced a serious threat "and the menace can be expected to extend to Southern Italy. No cases have yet been reported among the military forces, but the growing typhus rate is a potential menace to the Allied military effort."

15th | The San Juan earthquake devastated the province of San Juan in Argentina. Some 10,000 people were killed and one-third of the province's population was left homeless.

16th | Dwight D. Eisenhower formally assumed the duties of the Commander in Chief of the Allied Expeditionary Forces.

January

17th	A diplomatic incident occurred when The Soviet newspaper Pravda published a report claiming that representatives of Britain and Germany had met somewhere on the Iberian Peninsula to discuss making a separate peace. The British Foreign Office swiftly denied the rumour in an official message sent to the Soviet government.
18th	The Soviets broke the Siege of Leningrad by opening a narrow corridor south of Lake Ladoga.
19th	German submarine U-641 was depth charged and sunk in the Atlantic Ocean by the British corvette Violet.
21st	Australia and New Zealand signed the Canberra Pact, a treaty of mutual defence. The Canberra Pact, formally the Australian-New Zealand Agreement, also known as the ANZAC Pact, was a treaty of mutual co-operation between the governments of Australia and New Zealand, signed on 21 January 1944, following a conference that began on the 17th. The Pact was not a military alliance, but aimed to support Australian and New Zealand interests in the post-war world, particularly in the South Pacific. It was the "first clear and unmistakable statement of the two Dominion's post-war interests", and Alister McIntosh described it as having "said the right things in somewhat the wrong way".
22nd	President Roosevelt issued Executive Order 9417, creating the War Refugee Board to aid civilian victims of the Axis powers.
23rd	The Detroit Red Wings recorded the most lopsided win in National Hockey League history when they blew out the New York Rangers 15-0.

15   **0**

25th	Japanese destroyer Suzukaze was torpedoed and sunk northwest of Ponape by the American submarine Skipjack.
26th	Soviet forces captured Krasnogvardeisk near Leningrad. Two days later the city's pre-1923 name of Gatchina would be restored.
27th	The Red Army lifted the Siege of Leningrad after 2 years, 4 months, 2 weeks and 5 days.

January

29th	Koniuchy massacre: A unit of Soviet partisans accompanied by Jewish partisans killed at least 38 civilians in the village of Koniuchy in Nazi occupied Lithuania.
30th	Adolf Hitler made a radio address from his headquarters on the eleventh anniversary of the Nazis coming to power. He spent little time talking about the war situation and mostly spoke about Germany being Europe's only bulwark against communism.

February

1st	The French Forces of the Interior (FFI) was created, unifying all French Resistance movements.
2nd	The Battle of Narva began on the Eastern Front. The Battle for Narva Bridgehead began that day.
4th	German submarine U-854 struck a mine and sank in the Baltic Sea.
5th	In the Ukrainian sector, the Soviet 13th and 60th Armies captured Lutsk and Rovno.
6th	Over the night of February 6/7 some 200 Soviet bombers attacked Helsinki, the heaviest bombing of the Finnish capital since the war began.
7th	President Roosevelt asked Stalin not to allow the Polish border issue to undermine future international co-operation. Roosevelt proposed that the Polish Prime Minister accept the desired territorial changes and then be allowed to alter the makeup of his government without any evidence of foreign pressure.

8th	The German prisoner transport ship Petrella was sunk off Crete with the loss of 2,670 Italian POWs aboard.
9th	During the Battle of Anzio, German forces captured Aprilia from the British 1st Division which continued to hold "The Factory".
10th	The Japanese destroyer Minekaze was sunk south of Formosa by the American submarine Pogy.

February

11th	At the Anzio beachhead, German forces captured "The Factory" from the British 1st Division.
12th	The German steamboat Oria sank in a storm sailing from Rhodes to Piraeus with over 4,000 Italian prisoners of war aboard. It was one of the worst disasters of all time in the Mediterranean Sea.
13th	The Norwegian cargo ship Henry and passenger ship Irma were controversially sunk off Kristiansund by two ships of the Royal Norwegian Navy, who claimed the Irma and Henry were without lights or national markings.
14th	The United States declared neutrality in the border dispute between Poland and the Soviet Union.
16th	Stalin responded to Roosevelt's message of 7th February by saying the Polish government was made up of elements hostile to the Soviet Union and was incapable of friendly relations with the USSR. Stalin advised that "The basic improvement of the Polish government appears to be an urgent task."
17th	Operation Hailstone ended in United States victory. The Japanese lost 3 cruisers, 4 destroyers, 3 auxiliary cruisers, 2 submarine tenders, 3 smaller warships, 32 merchant ships and 270 aircraft at Truk. Operation Hailstone 17th –18th February 1944, was a massive United States Navy air and surface attack on Truk Lagoon conducted as part of the American offensive drive against the Imperial Japanese Navy (IJN) through the Central Pacific Ocean during World War II. Prior to Operation Hailstone, the IJN had used Truk as an anchorage for its large Combined Fleet. The coral atoll surrounding Truk's islands created a safe harbour where the few points of ingress and egress had been fortified by the Japanese with shore batteries, antiaircraft guns, and airfields.
18th	Operation Jericho: Allied aircraft raided Amiens prison in German-occupied France, breaching its walls and allowing 258 prisoners to escape.
19th	187 planes of the Luftwaffe bombed London as part of Operation Steinbock. It was the heaviest bombing of the British capital since May 1941.

February

20th | Erwin Rommel completed a four-day inspection tour of the Atlantic Wall. He reported to Adolf Hitler that the German coastal defences were up to all requirements.

22nd | The British oil tanker British Chivalry was sunk by Japanese submarine I-37 in the Indian Ocean. I-37 circled the sinking ship indiscriminately shooting at the survivors, for which Lieutenant-Commander Nakagawa Hajime was tried and found guilty of a war crime in 1948.

23rd | Claiming they helped the Nazis, Stalin exiled the vast majority of the Chechen and the Ingush population in the Caucasus to the deserts of Siberia and Central Asia.

24th | Finnish Prime Minister Edwin Linkomies announced that his country was ready to make peace.

27th | The U.S. Office of Strategic Services began Operation Ginny I with the objective of blowing up railway tunnels in Italy to cut German lines of communication, but the mission was aborted when the OSS team landed in the wrong place and could not locate the tunnel.

28th | German aviator Hanna Reitsch visited Hitler in Berchtesgaden to receive a second Iron Cross. While there she suggested the creation of a squad of suicide bombers who could fly specially designed versions of the V-1 flying bomb, and volunteered to become one such suicide pilot herself. Hitler was not receptive to the idea, believing it to be an inefficient use of resources, but he would investigate the prospect of designing such aircraft.

29th | The Battle of Ist was fought in the Adriatic Sea between Free French destroyers and a Kriegsmarine force. The result was a Free French victory as two German ships were sunk and one torpedo boat severely damaged.

March

1st | A massive strike began in the Italian Social Republic, for reasons that included resentment of producing for the Germans and the loyalty that many factory workers retained for Socialist and Communist ideologies. Estimates of the number of workers who participated in the strike range from 500,000 to 1.2 million.

March

2nd The 16th Academy Awards were held at Grauman's Chinese Theatre, marking the first time the ceremony was held in a large public venue. Casablanca won Best Picture. For the first time, winners for Best Supporting Actor and Best Supporting Actress were awarded full-size statuettes, instead of smaller-sized awards mounted on a plaque. This was the last year until 2009 to have 10 nominations for Best Picture

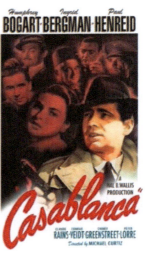

3rd In Rome, a protest of women, demanding the release of their husbands detained in a German station, ended tragically. Teresa Gullace, seven months pregnant, was killed by a German soldier while she tried to pass a sandwich to her husband. The story was later re-enacted in a famous episode of Rome open city.

4th The Philadelphia Phillies baseball team announced a uniform change for the coming season: the addition of a new sleeve patch depicting a blue jay perching atop the familiar "Phillies" lettering. The logo was the winning entry in a contest that received over 5,000 entries with a $100 war bond offered as a prize. Fans were confused because the Phillies did not actually officially change their name to Blue Jays, but this alternate nickname would never really catch on anyway and the blue jay sleeve patch was dropped in 1946.

5th Operation Thursday: The 77th Indian Infantry Brigade, otherwise known as the Chindits, flew by Hadrian glider from India into the heart of Burma.

6th Finland rejected a Soviet peace offer, objecting to the Soviet condition that all German troops in the country be interned and the 1940 borders be restored.

8th The war film The Purple Heart starring Dana Andrews and Richard Conte was released, dramatizing the "show trial" of a number of American airmen by the Japanese during World War II.

9th American destroyer escort Leopold was torpedoed and heavily damaged in the North Atlantic by German submarine U-255. The 28 survivors of the 191 crew were rescued and Leopold was abandoned to sink the next day.

10th The leftist Political Committee of National Liberation, commonly known as the "Mountain Government", was established in Greece.

March

11th — German military officer Eberhard von Breitenbuch took a concealed pistol to a military briefing with Hitler at the Berghof with the intention of assassinating him. However, SS guards barred Breitenbuch from the room where Hitler met with higher-ranking officers and so the assassination attempt never went forward.

13th — The Soviet 28th Army captured Kherson.

15th — During the Battle of Monte Cassino, the Allies dropped 992 tons of bombs on Monte Cassino Monastery and fired 195,000 rounds of artillery. British, Indian and New Zealand forces tried to storm the building but were unable to dislodge the Germans.

17th — Mount Vesuvius erupted, killing 26 civilians, destroying 88 American aircraft, and displacing 12,000 Italians.

18th — On the Modena Apennines, the 1st Fallschirm-Panzer Division Hermann Göring bombed the villages of Monchio, Susano and Costrignano, around Montefiorino, and slaughtered their whole population. The victims were 129, all civilians, and included women, old men and children. The carnage was aimed to repress the partisan activity in the zone.

19th — Eight German divisions carried out Operation Margarethe and occupied Hungary to forestall their Axis partner from making a separate peace with the Soviet Union.

21st — Finnish parliament held a secret session in which it rejected the peace terms offered by the Soviet Union.

22nd — Volcanic stones of all sizes from Mount Vesuvius began raining down from the sky, forcing the evacuation of airmen of 340th Bombardment Group stationed at an airfield a few miles from the volcano. Once Vesuvius subsided they returned to base and found that about 80 of their B-25 bombers had been destroyed by hot ash.

March

23rd	A bomb planted by Italian partisans killed 33 members of the SS in Rome.
24th	The "Great Escape" took place over the night of the 24th/25th, when 76 Royal Air Force prisoners of war escaped from Stalag Luft III in Lower Silesia.

25th	Stalag Luft III murders: Hitler ordered the execution of prisoners of war who were recaptured after escaping Stalag Luft III.
27th	A Finnish delegation met with Vyacheslav Molotov to discuss a peace settlement.
29th	The Japanese 31st Division cut the Imphal-Kohima road at Maram. The Imphal garrison could now only be supplied by air.
30th	The United States Navy began Operation Desecrate One, in which aircraft carriers launched attacks against Japanese bases on and around Palau. 36 Japanese ships were sunk or damaged in the attacks.
31st	Georg Lindemann replaced Walter Model as commander of Army Group North.

April

1st	The most significant bombing of Switzerland during World War II occurred when about 50 B-24s misidentified Schaffhausen as their target of Ludwigshafen and dropped bombs that resulted in 40 casualties.
2nd	The first Boeing B-29 Superfortress reached India after a long flight all the way from the United States through Britain and North Africa.
4th	Charlie Chaplin was acquitted by a federal court in Los Angeles of violating the Mann Act.
6th	German 1st Panzer Army forces in the Kamenets-Podolsky pocket completed their fighting withdrawal back to the German lines when they linked up with the 4th Panzer Army.
7th	Adolf Hitler suspended all laws in Berlin and made Joseph Goebbels the sole administrator of the city.
8th	The Germans began running long distance cargo flights between Polish airfields and Manchuria, flying Junkers Ju 290 A-9 aircraft at altitudes of up to 38,000 feet to cross the Soviet Union undetected.

April

9th — Charles de Gaulle became Commander-in-Chief of the Free French forces, ending a power struggle with Henri Giraud since the two men became co-presidents of the French Committee of National Liberation.

10th — General William Slim ordered a new offensive in Burma, calling for Stopford to break through to Kohima while the Imphal Garrison would make sorties into Japanese-held territory around them.

12th — German forces began withdrawing from the Crimea.

13th — The Montreal Canadiens defeated the Chicago Black Hawks 5-4 in overtime to win the Stanley Cup in a four-game sweep.

14th — The Bombay Explosion occurred in the Victoria Dock of Bombay when the freighter Fort Stikine caught fire and was destroyed in two giant blasts that killed about 800 people.

16th — Soviet forces cleared out the last pockets of German resistance at Yalta.

18th — The American submarine USS Gudgeon was bombed and sunk off Iwo Jima by a Japanese Mitsubishi G3M.

19th — Gérard Côté won the Boston Marathon, finishing just 13 seconds ahead of Johnny Kelley.

21st — Charles de Gaulle, leader of the French provisional government in Algiers, issued a simple decree giving French women the right to vote.

22nd — A two-day meeting between Hitler and Benito Mussolini began at Schloss Klessheim near Salzburg, also attended by Joachim von Ribbentrop, Wilhelm Keitel, Rudolf Rahn and Karl Wolff on the German side and Serafino Mazzolini, Rodolfo Graziani, Filippo Anfuso and general Umberto Morera for the Italians. Mussolini and his delegation presented a list of problems the Italian Social Republic was having which they attributed to the lack of cooperation with German authorities, but the German delegation no longer respected Mussolini who by now resembled a shadow of his former self.

23rd — The Salzburg conference between Hitler and Mussolini concluded. A compromise was reached in which Mussolini agreed to continue permitting Italian troops to be trained in Germany, with the best fighters allowed to form the nucleus of the new National Republican Army.

24th — The Billy Wilder-directed film noir Double Indemnity starring Fred MacMurray and Barbara Stanwyck was released.

April

25th Adolf Eichmann and the Nazis offered the Hungarian rescue worker Joel Brand the "Blood for Goods" deal, proposing that one million Jews be allowed to leave Hungary for any Allied-occupied country except Palestine, in exchange for goods obtained outside of Hungary. The deal would never be made because the Allies believed it to be a trick and the British press slammed it as blackmail.

27th The legislative assembly of the Canadian province of Quebec voted 55-4 to adopt a motion introduced by René Chaloult expressing disapproval of any attempt to send conscripted men overseas.

28th The first practice assault in Exercise Tiger, a series of large-scale rehearsals for D-Day, was held on Slapton Sands in Devon. The exercise was attacked by nine German E-boats that killed a total of 749 American servicemen. Two landing ships were sunk including USS LST-507.

29th In one of the worst friendly fire incidents of the war, Motor Torpedo Boat PT-346 was attacked off Rabaul by two American Marine Corsair planes that mistook two PT boats for Japanese gunboats. PT-346 was destroyed with nine men killed and nine wounded.

30th A U.S. task force of nine heavy cruisers and eight destroyers bombarded Japanese positions on Satawan.

May

2nd Spain bowed to pressure from the Allies and agreed to stop exporting tungsten to Germany.

3rd The American destroyer escort USS Donnell was torpedoed and heavily damaged in the Atlantic Ocean by German submarine U-473. Donnell was towed to Scotland and declared a total loss.

4th The mystery-thriller film Gaslight starring Charles Boyer, Ingrid Bergman, Joseph Cotten and Angela Lansbury (in her film debut) premiered in New York City.

5th After almost two years of internment in the Aga Khan's palace in Pune, Mahatma Gandhi was released for medical reasons. It would prove to be the last internment of Gandhi's life.

6th Soviet forces began their final attack on Sevastopol with a massive artillery bombardment.

8th The Czechoslovak government-in-exile signed a convention in London allowing the Soviet Army to liberate Czechoslovakia.

9th The Manhattan Ear, Nose and Throat and New York Hospitals opened the world's first eye bank.

11th Allied forces raided airfields and coastal installations in Normandy, hitting Calais particularly hard as part of the deception plan to make the Germans think the landings would be made there.

12th 19-year old Indian Sepoy Kamal Ram earned the Victoria Cross for his actions during his battalion's assault on the Gustav Line in Italy. Ram wiped out a German machine-gun post single-handedly, induced a second one to surrender and then assisted a companion in destroying a third.

13th The Germans completed their withdrawal from the Crimea, having evacuated more than 150,000 men by air and sea over several weeks.

May

14th	Vichy radio reported that French cardinals had appealed to the Roman Catholic clergy in Britain and the United States to use their influence to ensure that the French civilian population as well as towns, works of art and churches would be spared from Allied bombing as much as possible.
15th	Hungarian officials under the guidance of SS officials began deporting Jews from Hungary. By July 9 a total of about 440,000 Jews would be deported from the country, mostly to Auschwitz.

18th	Joseph Stalin ordered the deportation of the Crimean Tatars as a form of collective punishment for alleged collaboration with the Nazis.
20th	80 miles east of Warsaw, the Polish Resistance recovered a German V-2 rocket, dismantled it and sent it to London for analysis.
21st	The West Loch disaster occurred at the U.S. Naval Base in Pearl Harbour when a mortar round detonated aboard the LST-353, starting a fire that spread among ships being prepared for Operation Forager, the invasion of the Mariana Islands. Six LSTs were sunk and 163 naval personnel were killed.
22nd	This week's issue of Life magazine published a photo of a young American woman with a Japanese skull sent to her by her boyfriend in the U.S. Navy. Letters sent to the magazine widely condemned the publishing of the photo, and the Army directed its bureau of Public Relations to inform U.S. publishers that "the publication of such stories would be likely to encourage the enemy to take reprisals against American dead and prisoners of war."
23rd	A four-day constitutional referendum ended in Iceland. More than 98% of voters approved of the founding of the Republic of Iceland.
25th	Axis forces including the German XV Mountain Corps began Operation Rösselsprung, a combined airborne and ground assault on the headquarters of the Yugoslav Partisans in the Bosnian town of Drvar.
26th	Allied forces continued to advance toward Rome as American troops took Cori, the Canadians captured San Giovanni and the British took Monte Cairo.
27th	German submarine U-292 was depth charged and sunk west of Trondheim by a B-24 Liberator of No. 59 Squadron RAF.

May

29th | The Germans called off Operation Steinbock after four months of strategically bombing southern England accomplished little effect.

30th | Princess Charlotte of Monaco resigned her rights to the throne in favour of her son Prince Rainier.

31st | The Government of India announced the formation of a Department of Planning and Development to plan for the post-war period.

June

1st | The BBC broadcast a coded message based on the Paul Verlaine poem Chanson d'automne to inform the French Resistance that the invasion of France was imminent. The Germans understood the intent of the message but failed to bring up sufficient forces.

2nd | Representatives of the Soviet Union and Romania secretly met in Stockholm to discuss conditions for Romania's withdrawal from the war.

3rd | Asperger syndrome was identified for the first time, in a paper by the Austrian paediatrician Hans Asperger.

4th | Royal Air Force Meteorologist Group Captain James Stagg recommended that Overlord be postponed one day from June 5 to the 6th because of bad weather. Dwight D. Eisenhower followed his advice and postponed D-Day by 24 hours.

5th | The D-Day naval deceptions began. Allied ships and aircraft made deceptive movements in an attempt to deceive the Germans into believing that the Allied invasion force would land in the Calais region.

6th | D-Day: Operation Overlord commenced with the crossing of nearly 160,000 Allied troops over the English Channel to land on the beaches of Normandy, France.

7th | Actress Judy Garland divorced her husband of three years, songwriter David Rose, on grounds of general cruelty.

8th | The Battle of Port-en-Bessin ended in Allied victory.

June

9th	The Battle of Ushant was fought off the coast of Brittany between German and Allied destroyer flotillas. The result was an Allied victory as the Germans lost 2 destroyers.
10th	A Waffen-SS company carried out the Oradour-sur-Glane massacre in France, killing 642 residents of the village of Oradour-sur-Glane.
11th	In Normandy, the First United States Army captured Carentan and Lison.
12th	U.S. and British forces in Normandy linked up near Carentan, forming a solid 50-mile (80 km) battlefront with 326,000 men and 54,000 vehicles.
13th	RAF Bomber Command sent 221 aircraft to bomb Le Havre in its first daylight raid since May 1943. Three torpedo boats, fifteen S-boats, nine minesweepers and eight patrol boats were among the many German ships sunk in the raid.
14th	Eleanor Roosevelt, the First Lady of the United States, opened the White House Conference on How Women May Share in Post-War Policy-Making.
15th	The Co-operative Commonwealth Federation led by Tommy Douglas won the general election in the province of Saskatchewan, marking the first time a socialist government had been elected anywhere in Canada.
16th	The Treaty of Vis was signed in Yugoslavia, in an attempt by the Western Powers to merge the Yugoslav government in exile with the Communist Partisans fighting on the ground. The agreement provided for an interim government until the people could decide the post-war form of government in democratic elections.
17th	Iceland formally declared independence from Denmark.
18th	A V-1 flying bomb hit the Guards Chapel of Wellington Barracks during Sunday service and killed 121 people.
19th	A major storm in the English Channel destroyed large parts of the Mulberry harbours and shipping.

June

20th A V-2 rocket become the first man-made object in space during a test launch (MW 18014).

21st The British destroyer Fury struck a mine off Sword Beach, Normandy and was declared a total loss.

22nd The Appalachians tornado outbreak began in the Midwest and Middle Atlantic regions of the United States. Over 100 people were killed over the next two days, with Shinnston, West Virginia hit particularly hard as 66 fatalities were recorded in the town and surrounding area.

24th On the Normandy front the Germans deployed a new weapon—the unmanned Mistel aircraft.

25th The Bombardment of Cherbourg took place when U.S. and British warships attacked German fortifications in and around Cherbourg.

26th All three New York baseball teams (the Yankees, the Giants and the Dodgers) squared off at the Polo Grounds in an experimental round-robin exhibition game to raise money for war bonds. Each team would play in the field and bat for two consecutive innings, then sit for an inning until they had played a total of nine innings. The final score was Dodgers 5, Yankees 1, Giants 0.

28th Hitler sacked Ernst Busch as commander of Army Group Centre and replaced him with Walter Model.

30th Bush House, the headquarters of BBC World Service radio, was hit by a German flying bomb.

July

1st A counterattack by the German II SS Panzer Corps failed to dislodge the British Second Army around Caen. When Gerd von Rundstedt phoned Berlin to report the failure, Chief of Staff Wilhelm Keitel purportedly asked, "What shall we do?", to which Rundstedt replied, "Make peace, you fools! What else can you do?"

2nd The Razor's Edge by W. Somerset Maugham topped the New York Times Fiction Best Sellers list.

4th Canadian forces began Operation Windsor, an offensive to take Carpiquet.

6th Jackie Robinson was placed under arrest in quarters for refusing to move to the back of a military bus. He would be court-martialled but eventually acquitted in a trial on 2nd August.

7th Regent of Hungary Miklós Horthy ordered a stop to the deportation of Jews from the country. Even so, the Nazis declared all of Hungary except for Budapest free of Jews.

8th British and Canadian forces launched Operation Charnwood with the goal of at least partially capturing the city of Caen, which remained in German hands despite repeated attempts to take it over the past month.

10th Because of the danger of the German flying bombs, over 41,000 mothers and children left London in the second wartime exodus from the city and returned to their former wartime billets in the country.

11th The new German Tiger II heavy tank saw frontline combat for the first time during the Normandy campaign.

July

14th — Operation Ostra Brama ended in victory for the Polish Home Army when the German occupiers in Wilno were defeated, but the following day the Soviet NKVD entered the city and proceeded to intern the Polish fighters and arrest their officers.

16th — Adolf Hitler departed Berchtesgaden for what would be the final time as he flew to the Wolf's Lair.

17th — German field marshal Erwin Rommel was seriously wounded when a Spitfire strafed his staff car near Livarot. Numerous Allied pilots claimed credit for the attack that knocked Rommel out of the war, but following the 2004 publicization of a Canadian historian's research into the incident, the Canadian Forces officially attribute the feat to Charley Fox of the RCAF.

20th — 20 July Plot: An attempt was made to assassinate Adolf Hitler, perpetrated by Claus von Stauffenberg and other conspirators within the German military. At 12:42 p.m. during a conference at the Wolf's Lair, a bomb that Stauffenberg had concealed inside a briefcase went off, killing a stenographer and leaving three officers near death. The others in the room, including Hitler himself, were wounded but survived.

21st — At 1 a.m., Hitler gave a speech over the radio to prove to the German people that he was still alive. He declared that the conspirators would be "exterminated quite mercilessly."

22nd — Majdanek concentration camp was liberated by the Red Army, the first concentration camp to be liberated by Allied forces. The Soviet advance was so rapid that the SS fled before evidence of what went on in the camp could be destroyed. When Soviet officials invited journalists to the site, the full extent of Nazi atrocities began to be known to the world.

23rd — Heinrich Himmler launched a manhunt to catch the conspirators in the 20 July Bomb Plot.

25th — Operation Gaff: Six British commandos parachuted into German-occupied Orléans, France with the aim of killing or kidnapping German field marshal Erwin Rommel. When they learned that Rommel had already been injured they moved toward advancing U.S. Army lines on foot.

26th — President Roosevelt gathered his Pacific commanders at Pearl Harbour for a two-day conference on strategy in the Pacific. Douglas MacArthur supported an advance on the Philippines while Chester Nimitz argued for making Formosa the first priority. Roosevelt listened impartially and made no decision at the time.

28th — The rocket-powered German Messerschmitt Me 163 Komet fighter plane saw its first active combat.

July

29th | Radio Moscow broadcast appeals from Polish communists for Warsaw to rise up against the German occupiers.

30th | During the Battle of Normandy, the British Army began Operation Bluecoat with the goal of capturing Vire and Mont Pinçon.

31st | Soviet forces in the north reached the Gulf of Riga, cutting off German Army Group North, which could now only be resupplied by sea.

August

1st | The Prague resistance Home Army began the Warsaw Uprising against Nazi occupation forces.

2nd | SS authorities in Auschwitz-Birkenau murdered the last residents (just under 3,000) of the so-called Gypsy family camp.

3rd | The Education Act 1944 received Royal Assent in the United Kingdom. The Education Act 1944 made major changes in the provision and governance of secondary schools in England and Wales. It is also known as the "Butler Act" after the President of the Board of Education, R. A. Butler. Historians consider it a "triumph for progressive reform," and it became a core element of the post-war consensus supported by all major parties. The Act was repealed in steps with the last parts repealed in 1996.

4th | In Amsterdam, the family of Anne Frank was discovered, seized and deported by the Nazis.

5th | The Cowra breakout occurred when over 1,100 Japanese prisoners of war attempted to escape from a POW camp near Cowra in New South Wales, Australia. Four Australian soldiers and 231 Japanese were killed, but hundreds managed to escape although they would all be recaptured within ten days.

8th | The Damasta sabotage occurred near the Cretan village of Damasta. Greek resistance fighters led by British Special Operations Executive Officer W. Stanley Moss attacked Axis occupation forces and killed 35 Germans and 10 Italians.

9th | The first poster depicting Smokey Bear, a mascot created to educate the American public about the dangers of forest fires, was released.

11th | German submarine U-385 was depth charged and sunk in the Bay of Biscay by a Short Sunderland of No. 461 Squadron RAAF and by the British sloop Starling.

12th | Operation Pluto: The world's first undersea oil pipeline was laid between England and France.

14th | The Fort Lawton Riot began at Fort Lawton in Seattle. An Italian prisoner of war was killed during a violent conflict between American soldiers and Italian POWs.

17th | VIII Corps of the Third United States Army took Saint-Malo when the German-held fortress there surrendered after enduring two weeks of bombing and shelling

18th | The German 7th Army retreated across the Orne, leaving 18,000 men behind to be captured.

August

19th | The Battle for Paris began. Resistance fighters in the capital became confident enough to begin making sniper attacks on nervous German troops.

20th | German submarine U-188 was scuttled in Bordeaux to prevent capture by the Allies, one of five U-boats lost that day. U-9 was sunk at Constanta in a Soviet air raid, U-413 was lost to a naval mine in the Cornish corridor, U-984 was sunk by Canadian warships in the Bay of Biscay and U-1229 was sunk in the Atlantic Ocean by Allied aircraft.

21st | The British comedy-drama film A Canterbury Tale starring Eric Portman, Sheila Sim and Dennis Price premiered in the United Kingdom.

22nd | Nazi occupation forces in Greece began the Holocaust of Kedros. Over the next several days nine villages in the Amari Valley in Crete would be razed and looted and 164 Greek civilians killed.

23rd | The Battle of Audierne Bay was fought between German and Allied naval flotillas. The result was an Allied victory as eight German ships were sunk.

August

24th   The Harvard Mark I electro-mechanical computer, developed and built by IBM, was formally presented to Harvard University. The Harvard Mark I, or IBM Automatic Sequence Controlled Calculator (ASCC), was a general-purpose electromechanical computer used in the war effort during the last part of World War II. One of the first programs to run on the Mark I was initiated on 29th March 1944 by John von Neumann. At that time, von Neumann was working on the Manhattan Project, and needed to determine whether implosion was a viable choice to detonate the atomic bomb that would be used a year later. The Mark I also computed and printed mathematical tables, which had been the initial goal of British inventor Charles Babbage for his "analytical engine" in 1837. The Mark I was disassembled in 1959, but portions of it were displayed in the Science Centre as part of the Harvard Collection of Historical Scientific Instruments until being moved to the new Science and Engineering Complex in Allston, Massachusetts in July 2021. Other sections of the original machine had much earlier been transferred to IBM and the Smithsonian Institution.

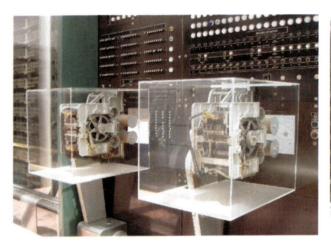 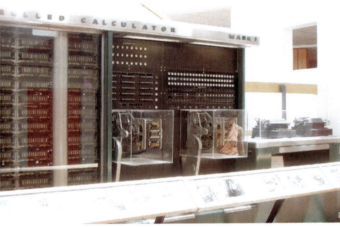

25th   The Battle for Paris ended at 2:30 p.m. when the German commander Dietrich von Choltitz surrendered the French capital. At 4 p.m. Charles de Gaulle arrived in the city and walked amid a cheering crowd to the Hôtel de Ville, where he made a rousing speech.

26th   Charles de Gaulle headed a liberation parade in Paris, laying a wreath at the Tomb of the Unknown Soldier and ceremonially relighting the eternal flame at the Arc de Triomphe, then marching along the Champs-Élysées to attend a service at Notre Dame to give thanks for the liberation of the city. Sniper fire rang out during the parade, which de Gaulle ignored.

29th   Allied commanders turned over the administration of Paris to Charles de Gaulle and the French Committee of National Liberation.

30th   Soviet forces entered the important oil centre of Ploiești, Romania. The city had been heavily bombed by the British and Americans in the Oil Campaign and only five refineries producing just 20 percent of normal production were active.

31st   The 53rd Army of the 2nd Ukrainian Front entered Bucharest.

September

1st   The First Canadian Army captured Dieppe, the site of the failed 1942 commando raid, and pressed on along the northern French coast.

September

2nd	German submarine U-394 was sunk southeast of Jan Mayen by a Fairey Swordfish of 825 Squadron, Fleet Air Arm and gunfire from British warships.
3rd	Finland and the Soviet Union agreed on a ceasefire to take effect at 8:00 a.m. the next morning.
5th	The Cornwall–Massena earthquake along the Saint Lawrence rift system in North America did $2 million damage.
6th	All four carrier groups of Task Force 38 began air strikes on Japanese positions in the Palau Islands.
7th	Members of Vichy France's collaborationist government were relocated to Germany where an enclave was established for them in Sigmaringen Castle.
8th	The Italian ocean liner Rex was sunk at Trieste by an air raid of Bristol Beau fighters from No. 272 Squadron RAF.

10th	The U.S. 3rd Armoured Division occupied St. Vith and reached the German border.
11th	US troops cross the border into Nazi Germany for the first time. At 16:30 hours, a 7-person patrol led by Sgt. Warner W. Holzinger of the 2nd Platoon, Troop B, 85th Cavalry Reconnaissance Squadron, 5th Armoured Division, crossed the river Our at Stolzembourg, Luxembourg and reached Keppeshausen. They studied the pillbox area, and returned safely to Stolzembourg at 18:50 having encountered no German military personnel. This was also the first advance through enemy lines in Germany.
12th	Romania signed an armistice with the Allies in Moscow. Romania agreed to provide twelve divisions to fight Germany, provide goods and raw materials to the USSR, ban all fascist organizations, repeal anti-Jewish laws and revert to their 1940 borders. The Soviet Union took control of Bessarabia and northern Bukovina.
13th	Soviet aircraft began dropping supplies to the Home Army in Warsaw overnight.
14th	The Soviets began the Baltic Offensive and the Riga Offensive.
15th	The Germans carried out Operation Tanne Ost to capture the Finnish island of Suursaari before it could fall into Soviet hands. The operation was a complete failure for the Germans with the Finns taking 1,231 prisoners.

September

16th	Hitler made the decision to go through with the Ardennes Offensive in his Prussian headquarters (the Wolf's Lair). This would become the Battle of the Bulge.
17th	30,000 Dutch rail workers obeyed a call from General Eisenhower to go on strike to paralyze the German transport system in Holland. Many of the workers went into hiding.
18th	American B-17 bombers dropped 1,284 containers of supplies to the Home Army in Warsaw, but only 228 fell on Polish-controlled territory. This was the only major supply drop of the war that the Soviets allowed the western Allies to carry out.
19th	SS and Police Leader of Denmark Günther Pancke proclaimed a state of emergency and ordered the Danish police disarmed in an effort to stop the Danish transportation strike from becoming a general strike. This measure brought about shooting in front of the castle in Copenhagen when the royal guards thought they would be disarmed as well, and eight people were killed. Striking would continue for two more days.
20th	The pirate film Frenchman's Creek starring Joan Fontaine and Arturo de Córdova was released.
21st	The St. Louis Cardinals clinched their third straight National League pennant with a 5–4 win over the Boston Braves in the first game of a doubleheader.
22nd	Operation Wellhit ended in Allied victory when Boulogne fell to the 3rd Canadian Division. Operation Undergo now began with the objective of taking the French port of Calais.
23rd	U.S. President Franklin D. Roosevelt made a campaign speech in Washington before the International Teamsters Brotherhood. He responded to a rumour that he'd sent a Navy destroyer to the Aleutian Islands to retrieve his Scottish Terrier Fala at great taxpayer expense by saying, "You know, Fala is Scotch, and being a Scottie, as soon as he learned that the Republican fiction writers in Congress and out had concocted a story that I had left him behind on the Aleutian Islands and had sent a destroyer back to find him— at a cost to the taxpayers of two or three, or eight or twenty million dollars- his Scotch soul was furious. He has not been the same dog since. I am accustomed to hearing malicious falsehoods about myself—such as that old, worm-eaten chestnut that I have represented myself as indispensable. But I think I have a right to resent, to object to libellous statements about my dog." Roosevelt drew huge laughs from the audience and the speech became a defining moment in the campaign.
24th	German submarine U-596 was bombed and damaged in Salamis Bay by American aircraft and consequently scuttled.
25th	Operation Market Garden ended in defeat for the Allies when they failed to cross the Rhine. The operation was mostly overlooked in popular histories of World War II until the 1974 publication of the book A Bridge Too Far by Cornelius Ryan, which was the basis for a film of the same name released in 1977.
26th	The Battle of Arnhem ended in German victory. After nine days of fighting, the remnants of the division were withdrawn in Operation Berlin. The Allies were unable to advance further with no secure bridges over the Nederrijn and the front-line stabilised south of Arnhem. The British 1st Airborne Division lost nearly three quarters of its strength and did not see combat again.

September

27th	The Japanese troop transport and hospital ship Ural Maru was torpedoed and sunk in the South China Sea by the American submarine Flasher with the loss of some 2,000 lives.
28th	A roundup in Bratislava orchestrated by Alois Brunner captures 1,800 Jews and puts an end to one of the most successful underground Jewish organizations during the Holocaust, the Bratislava Working Group. The Jews are deported to Auschwitz, where most are murdered.
29th	The Red Army began the Moonsund Landing Operation, an amphibious assault as part of the Baltic Offensive.
30th	The besieged German garrison at Calais surrendered to Canadian forces.

October

1st	The St. Louis Browns won the American League pennant on the final day of the season by beating the New York Yankees 5-2. The Browns, who had never won a pennant in franchise history and would not win another as a St. Louis team, were helped immensely by the wartime roster depletion across baseball that happened to affect them less than the other ballclubs. The average major league team had ten 4-F players on its roster, but the Browns had eighteen.

2nd	The Warsaw Uprising was put down after two months by Nazi occupation forces.
3rd	The American submarine USS Seawolf went missing, probably sunk in the Molucca Sea by the U.S. destroyer escort Richard M. Rowell in a friendly fire accident.
4th	German submarines U-92, U-228 and U-437 were all sunk or rendered inoperable by an air raid on Bergen by RAF aircraft.
5th	Joseph Goebbels announced a reduction in food rations.
6th	Milan Nedić, president of the Serbian collaborationist puppet state of the Axis powers, the Government of National Salvation, fled from Belgrade in Nazi-occupied Serbia by air together with other Serbian collaborators and German officials, via Hungary to Austria.
7th	"You Always Hurt the One You Love" by The Mills Brothers topped the Billboard singles charts.

October

8th | Battle of the Nijmegen salient ended - the Germans were unable to recover lost ground taken by the Allies during Operation Market Garden.

9th | The Fourth Moscow Conference began. Winston Churchill, Joseph Stalin and U.S. ambassador W. Averell Harriman met to discuss the future of Europe.

10th | In Genoa, the explosion of a German ammunition deposit in the San Benigno quarter (caused by lightning or, according to some never confirmed theories, by a partisan attack) caused hundreds of deaths. The victims included German soldiers, Genoese civilians living in the area and refugees in air-raid shelters.

11th | A secret Hungarian delegation signed a ceasefire agreement in Moscow. Hungary agreed to declare war on Germany and give up all territory gained since 1937.

12th | Canadian Arctic explorer Henry Larsen reached Vancouver after sailing from Halifax, Nova Scotia through the Northwest Passage in just 86 days.

13th | The Germans launched V-1 and V-2 flying bombs at Antwerp in an attempt to deny use of its crucial port to the Allies.

14th | In Italy, the American Fifth Army had some success on the Apennine front; a South African division entered Grizzana, and the German Army left Livergnano. In Romagna, the Polish II Corps went into action.

15th | The ceasefire between Hungary and the Soviet Union was publicized. Regent of Hungary Miklós Horthy made a radio broadcast announcing that he had made a separate peace with the Soviet Union withdrawing Hungary from the war. Germans respond immediately with Operation Panzerfaust.

16th | American bombing of Salzburg destroys the dome of the city's cathedral and most of a Mozart family home.

October

17th	Contact was lost with the USS Escolar. The American submarine was probably lost to a mine in the Yellow Sea.
18th	Erwin Rommel was given a state funeral in Ulm. German military personnel and Nazi officials who attended included Friedrich Ruge, Karl Strölin, Konstantin von Neurath and Wilhelm Ritter von Leeb.
19th	The Cuba-Florida Hurricane made landfall at Sarasota, Florida and moved north. A total of 300 people was killed in the storm.
21st	Despite heavy rain, U.S. President Franklin D. Roosevelt rode in an open car through 51 miles (82 km) of New York City streets on his way to make a speech at Ebbets Field in Brooklyn. With a little over two weeks left to go in the presidential election campaign, Roosevelt's ride through the city in the pouring rain without any proper covering was an attempt to show that he was still healthy.
22nd	Canadian Private Ernest Smith earned the Victoria Cross for his actions over the night of October 21–22 on the Savio in Italy. Smith disabled a German tank and then killed four panzer grenadiers and damaged another tank while protecting a wounded comrade.

24th	The Japanese hell ship Arisan Maru was torpedoed and sunk in the South China Sea by an American submarine. Only nine of the 1,781 Allied and civilian prisoners of war survived.
26th	The Battle of Leyte Gulf ended in decisive Allied victory. On the final day of the battle the Japanese lost the cruisers Abukuma, Kinu and Noshiro, destroyers Hayashimo, Nowaki and Uranami and submarine I-26.
27th	The Japanese destroyers Fujinami and Shiranui were sunk north of Oloilo, Panay by U.S. aircraft.

October

28th | A V-1 flying bomb killed 71 people in Antwerp.

29th | Reichsführer SS Heinrich Himmler orders the closure of gas chambers at Auschwitz and other extermination camps.

30th | The U.S. Third Army completed the capture of Maizières-lès-Metz.

31st | The last German forces evacuated Salonika ahead of the arrival of a force of the British Special Boat Service. German vessels in the port were also scuttled, removing the last Kriegsmarine presence in the Aegean Sea.

November

1st | 1 November 1944 reconnaissance sortie over Japan: An American F-13 Superfortress conducted the first flight by Allied aircraft over Japan since the Doolittle Raid of April 1942.

2nd | 50,000 of Budapest's Jews were sent on a forced march to Austria. 10,000 would die over the six-day march. Moscow requested permission for their troops to enter Bulgarian territory.

3rd | Japanese destroyer Akikaze was torpedoed and sunk west of Cape Bolinao, Philippines by the American submarine Pintado when she intercepted torpedoes intended for the aircraft carrier Jun'yō.

6th | The provisional government of France struck down all of the country's anti-Semitic laws. Implementation of this measure was difficult when it came to returning Jews to their former occupations and giving them back their homes and confiscated property.

7th | The Air battle over Niš occurred over Niš, Serbia between the Air Forces of the United States and the Soviet Union. For an unknown reason, American P-38s attacked Soviet ground troops and then came under attack themselves from Yak fighters of the Soviet Air Force. It is unclear exactly what happened or why, since documents related to the incident apparently remain classified in both countries.

10th | Nazi occupation forces in the Netherlands began a two-day roundup of 50,000 men in Rotterdam to be sent to Germany for forced labour.

11th | The 1942–44 musicians' strike finally ended in the United States when RCA Victor and Columbia Records finally capitulated to the union's demands.

12th | 80,000 leftists demonstrated in Rome in celebration of the anniversary of the Bolshevik Revolution and denounced the monarchy.

13th | The Japanese destroyers Akebono, Akishimo, Hatsuharu and Kiso were all bombed and sunk by U.S. Navy aircraft in and around the Cavite Naval Yard in Manila, while destroyer Okinami was sunk 8 nautical miles west of the city.

14th | Nazi resistance members Walter Cramer, Bernhard Letterhaus and Ferdinand von Lüninck were hanged at Plötzensee Prison in Berlin.

15th	Japanese landing craft depot ship Akitsu Maru was torpedoed and sunk in the Korea Strait by the submarine USS Queenfish, killing over 2,000.
17th	While part of convoy Hi-81, the Japanese landing craft depot ship Mayasan Maru was sunk in the East China Sea by the American submarine Picuda. Some 3,856 lives were lost in one of the highest maritime casualty counts of the war.
18th	More Fun Comics issue #101 was published (cover date Jan-Feb), featuring the first appearance of Super boy.

19th	The American submarine Sculpin was scuttled off Truk after being damaged by Japanese destroyer Yamagumo.
20th	Adolf Hitler left his Eastern Front headquarters, the Wolfsschanze ("Wolf's Lair"), for the last time as the Red Army approached the borders of Germany.
22nd	Canadian Parliament assembled in a special meeting to debate the conscription crisis. Prime Minister William Lyon Mackenzie King said that it had not become necessary to require drafted troops to serve overseas and that to do so "would occasion the most serious controversy that could arise in Canada. I can think of no course fraught with greater danger to our war effort, to say nothing of the unity and strength of Canada today and for generations to come, than a general election at this late stage of the war on the conscription issue. Until it is apparent conscription for overseas forces is necessary, the government would not be justified in taking the risk of widespread national dissention."
24th	The Terrace Mutiny began when Canadian soldiers based in Terrace, British Columbia began disobeying orders and seizing weapons after hearing rumours that conscripts might be deployed overseas. The mutiny was largely censored by authorities and it did not come to be well known by the general public.
25th	German submarine U-482 was sunk west of Shetland by the Royal Navy frigate Ascension.

November

26th	Heinrich Himmler ordered the destruction of the crematoria at Auschwitz concentration camp to eliminate evidence of the mass killings there.
27th	The Norwegian prisoner ship Rigel was bombed and sunk in the Norwegian Sea by Fairey Barracuda aircraft of the Fleet Air Arm. 2,571 people were killed.
28th	The 57th Army of the 3rd Ukrainian Front captured the Hungarian town of Mohács.
29th	Japanese aircraft carrier Shinano was torpedoed and sunk southeast of Kushimoto by the American submarine Archerfish.
30th	The 53rd Army of the 2nd Ukrainian Front took the Hungarian city of Eger.

December

2nd	The Army–Navy Game was played at Baltimore Municipal Stadium, with Army defeating Navy 23-7 before a crowd of 66,659. About 30,000 members of the general public were allowed to attend on the conditions of living within 8.3 miles of Baltimore and purchasing a $25 war bond. General Douglas MacArthur sent Army head coach Earl Blaik a congratulatory telegram after the game.
3rd	A series of clashes in Athens known as the Dekemvriana ("December events") began when British troops and Greek police opened fire on a massive leftist demonstration, killing 28 and wounding 100.
4th	Dutch famine of 1944: German occupation authorities in the Netherlands cut the bread ration to two pounds per person per week.

6th	The Germans began removing all the electric trains in the Netherlands along with their wiring and sending them to Germany to replace the train system in places where it had been destroyed by Allied bombing.
8th	Iwo Jima suffered the heaviest U.S. air raid of the Pacific War.
9th	German submarine U-862 shelled the Greek tanker SS Illios off the southern South Australian coast.

December

10th Nobel Prizes were awarded for the first time since 1939. Since the customary ceremonies still could not be held in Stockholm because of the war, a special luncheon was held under the auspices of The American-Scandinavian Foundation at the Waldorf Astoria hotel in New York City. The Award in Physics went to Isidor Isaac Rabi (United States), Chemistry to Otto Hahn (Germany), Physiology or Medicine to Joseph Erlanger and Herbert Spencer Gasser (United States), Literature to Johannes V. Jensen (Denmark) and the Peace Prize to the International Committee of the Red Cross. Three retroactive recipients for 1943 were also named, in accordance with the Nobel Foundation's statutes allowing the awards to be reserved for one year. They were Otto Stern of the United States for Physics, George de Hevesy (Germany) for Chemistry and Carl Peter Henrik Dam (Denmark) and Edward Adelbert Doisy (United States) for Physiology or Medicine.

11th Kia Motors founded in South Korea (then Japanese rule Korea), as predecessor name was Kyungsung Precision Industry in Seoul.

12th The U.S. Third Army captured the V-rocket factory at Wittring in eastern France.

13th American cruiser Nashville was severely damaged off Negros Island by a kamikaze attack and required four months of repairs.

14th At least 186 Japanese aircraft were deployed for an all-out attack on the American invasion force sailing toward Mindoro. Most of them failed to locate the American convoys and at least 46 were shot down.

15th During the Battle of Mindoro, the Sixth United States Army landed on Mindoro itself. The Japanese offered weak opposition on the ground but continued to respond strongly in the air, sending a wave of kamikazes to the battle zone that managed to destroy a pair of LSTs.

16th Benito Mussolini gave a speech at the Teatro Lirico in Milan that would be his last. Although he maintained that new German weapons would turn the tide of the war, it was clearly a political last will and testament as he tried to defend himself in the eyes of history and presented a dark picture of a Bolshevik Europe in the event of Allied victory.

17th The U.S. military began preparations for deploying nuclear weapons by activating the 509th Composite Group.

18th Douglas MacArthur was made a five-star general in the U.S. Army.

19th German forces captured 9,000 surrounded U.S. troops in the Schnee Eifel region on the Belgian-German border and pushed the Americans back off German soil.

20th Dwight D. Eisenhower was made a five-star general in the U.S. Army.

21st The Walt Disney animated musical film The Three Caballeros premiered in Mexico City.

22nd U.S. General Anthony McAuliffe responded to a German command to surrender the besieged garrison at Bastogne with a brief reply centred on a full sheet of paper: "N U T S!"

23rd In the Battle of the Bulge, the U.S. First Army withdrew from St. Vith while III Corps of the Third Army moved north to relieve the siege of Bastogne.

December

24th — Mosquito Bowl took place on Guadalcanal; "The Mosquito Bowl, A Game of Life and Death in World War II" by Buzz Bissinger. The Mosquito Bowl was a football game played December 24, 1944 between two regiments of Marines at Guadalcanal during World War II. Buzz Bissinger in 2022 wrote an account, The Mosquito Bowl: A Game of Life and Death in World War II, which was widely reviewed. Members of the 6th Marine Division, many of whom had played college football, were training on Guadalcanal during the final months of 1944. Many had been named to all-conference or all-American teams. Both of the division's 4th and 29th regiments could field a team of such prominent players, and a game was organized for Christmas Eve with sixty-five players, including John McLaughry and Tony Butkovich. The game ended with a scoreless tie.

25th — The British frigate HMS Dakins was severely damaged by a mine off Ostend and rendered a constructive total loss.

26th — German submarine U-486 torpedoed the British frigates Affleck and Capel in the English Channel off Cherbourg. Affleck was declared a constructive total loss and Capel was sunk.

27th — The Siege of Bastogne ended in American victory.

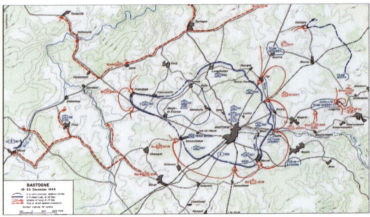

28th — Hockey star Maurice Richard of the Montreal Canadiens showed up exhausted to the Montreal Forum after spending the day helping his family move from one apartment to another. That night he recorded eight points (five goals and three assists) during a 9–2 win over the Detroit Red Wings, a new NHL record for points by one player in a single game that stood until 1976.

29th — German submarine U-322 was depth charged and sunk south of Weymouth, Dorset by Canadian corvette Calgary.

30th — General Leslie Groves, director of the Manhattan Project, reported that an atomic bomb equivalent to 10,000 tons of TNT would be ready for testing by the summer of 1945.

31st — The Grumman F8F Bearcat entered service with the United States Navy.

PEOPLE IN POWER

John Curtin
1941-1945
Australia
Prime Minister

Philippe Pétain
1940-1944
France
Président

Getúlio Vargas
1930-1945
Brazil
President

William Mackenzie
1935-1948
Canada
Prime Minister

Lin Sen
1943-1948
China
Government of China

Adolf Hitler
1934-1945
Germany
Führer of Germany

Lord Wavell
1944-1947
India
Viceroy of India

Benito Mussolini
1922-1945
Italy
President

Hirohito
1926-1989
Japan
Emperor

Manuel Ávila Camacho
1940-1946
Mexico
President

Joseph Stalin
1922-1952
Russia
Premier

Jan Smuts
1939-1948
South Africa
Prime Minister

Franklin D. Roosevelt
1933-1945
United States
President

Hubert Pierlot
1939-1945
Belgium
Prime Minister

Peter Fraser
1939-1949
New Zealand
Prime Minister

Sir Winston Churchill
1940-1945
United Kingdom
Prime Minister

Per Albin Hansson
1936-1946
Sweden
Prime Minister

Christian X
1912-1947
Denmark
King

Francisco Franco
1936-1975
Spain
President

Miklós Horthy
1920-1944
Hungary
Kingdom of Hungary

**The Year You Were Born 1944
Book by Sapphire Publishing
All rights reserved**